TOPICS
IN HOME
ECONOMICS

# FOOD SCIENCE & TECHNOLOGY

Anita Tull

Oxford University Press 1989

Oxford University Press, Walton Street, Oxford OX2 6DP

*Oxford New York Toronto*
*Delhi Bombay Calcutta Madras Karachi*
*Petaling Jaya Singapore Hong Kong Tokyo*
*Nairobi Dar es Salaam Cape Town*
*Melbourne Auckland*

and associated companies in
*Ibadan Berlin*

*Oxford* is a trademark of Oxford University Press



ISBN 0 19 832758 7

**Acknowledgements**

Illustrations are by Helen Charlton, Oxford Illustrators, Nigel Paige.

Cover illustration is by Barbara Mullarney-Wright.

The publisher would like to thank the following for permission to reproduce their photographs:

Ace Photo Agency p58 right; Biophoto Associates p17 far left; G. C. Cook, Hospital for Tropical Diseases p17 middle left, far right; Farmers Weekly p13; Sally & Richard Greenhill p11 middle; Holt Studios Ltd p11 left, right; Rob Judges p7 left, p14 both, p28, p35 both, p45 all, p53 all, p60 all; Janet MacKenzie, Clinical Research Centre p38 all; Bill Meadows p58 left; National Medical Slide Bank p17 middle right, p40; J. Sainsbury's Archives p7 right, p43 all; Anita Tull p51.

The graph on page 41 is reproduced with permission from *Yours for Life*, a dental health education programme © Colgate Palmolive Ltd, and the table on page 57 from *New Home Economics*, September 1986, Forbes Publications.

The author would like to thank Zena and Nathalie.

Designed by Raynor Design

Set by Tradespools Ltd, Frome, Somerset

Printed in Great Britain

**Scores for quiz on page 62**

| | |
|---|---|
| **1** A 0, B 1, C 3 | **4** A 0, B 1, C 3 |
| **2** A 3, B 1, C 0 | **5** A 0, B 1, C 3 |
| **3** A 0, B 1, C 3 | **6** A 0, B 1, C 3 |

Add up your total score.
How did you rate?

12–18 Good. You are generally aware of different aspects of the food you buy and eat.

6–12 Fair. You could become a better consumer by becoming more familiar with food labels, prices, and what is available.

0–5 Poor! You need to go shopping, read labels, and find out more about your food.

**Answer to word search on page 63**

1 fertilizers
2 omnivores
3 pasteurization
4 hydrogenation
5 label
6 fortification
7 dextrose
8 fast food
9 packaging
10 manufacturer
11 protein
12 emulsifier
13 salt
14 sun
15 organic

# Contents

**Introduction** *4*
The food industry *5*
Food investigations *8*

**Where does food come from?** *10*
Food production *12*
Growing plant crops *13*
Food surpluses *15*
What do plants need to grow? *16*

**Processing food** *18*
Nutrition labels *20*
The nutritional value of processed food *22*
Food manufacturers and nutrition *23*
Food additives *24*
Water in food *28*

**Food and health** *30*
Fat in food – what do you need to know? *31*
Sugar in food – what do you need to know? *34*
Salt in food – what do you need to know? *37*
Fibre in food – what do you need to know? *38*
Dental health *40*

**Food for today's consumer** *42*
Designing food *42*
Fast food *46*

**Preparing and cooking food** *48*
Changes in foods during preparation *49*
Changes in foods during cooking *52*
Efficiency in the kitchen *56*

**The end of the food chain** *58*
Packaging *58*
Wasting food *61*

**Quiz** – How do you rate as a food consumer? *62*
**Word search** *63*
**Index** *64*

# Introduction

Today's food is different in many ways from the food our ancestors ate. The large variety available (if you live in a wealthy country), and the ways in which foods are prepared for selling and eating, reflect the many changes that have taken place in our style of living.

▷ Think of some foods that are now available, as a result of the following examples of developments and changes in life style:

1 More women go out to work.
2 Plastics are widely used
3 More people visit countries overseas.
4 Transport is available almost everywhere.
5 Technological developments have led to changes in the home and in industry.

Think of other changes in life style and foods to go with them. ◁

Consumers (people who buy and eat food) are better informed about the composition and sale of the food they buy, and they are also protected by law. However, it is up to each person to read the information and put it to use, and it is the job of the food industry to make that information clear and correct.

This book aims to encourage **you** to think about and seek out information about your food, to help you make wise and responsible choices. It covers a variety of topics of current concern and interest about food, and follows the food from its origins to its disposal.

Throughout the book, where appropriate, scientific explanations are given for specific topics. Some people are 'put off' by anything scientific, but the aim is to help explain some of the words that are used on food labels by manufacturers and nutritionists, and to help you to understand what happens to food when it is produced, processed, cooked and eaten.

Each topic covered in the book includes a variety of activities to be undertaken individually or as a group. These consist of Things to do (surveys, observations, questions) and Investigations (practical and written). To help you to gain the most knowledge from these activities, try to follow the advice given below:

1 Use a variety of sources of information, e.g. books, leaflets, newspaper articles, manufacturers, food associations, health education centres, your own observations, etc.
2 Write answers, comments, conclusions, etc., **in your own words**, using the information you have found out.
3 Select the information you use carefully – make sure it is relevant to (applies to) the topic you are studying.

# The food industry

The food industry is a vast and complex organization. Thousands of people are employed in it, from waiters and farm labourers to food scientists and managing directors of large supermarket chains. You probably have most contact with the food industry at the consumption end, or you may actually have a part time job in it. The main groups of people whose job it is to produce, prepare, sell, and monitor your food are given below.

**Food growers (producers)**
Other people involved include:
- farm machinery technologists
- veterinary surgeons and health inspectors
- agricultural scientists and advisors
- genetic engineers (help produce better crops, healthier animals)
- animal feed and fertilizer producers and suppliers

**Food manufacturers**
Other people involved include:
- food scientists and technologists (who deal with mass production of food, its composition and standards, and the development of new products)
- food packagers
- food transporters
- food advertisers
- food inspectors

**Food wholesalers and retailers**
(Wholesalers supply shops, retailers supply consumers.) Other people involved include:
- health inspectors
- buyers (who decide which foods to sell in a particular shop)
- shop workers

**Food caterers**
Other people involved include:
- managers and workers in canteens, restaurants, fast food outlets, etc.
- health inspectors

**Nutritionists and dieticians**
who advise at all levels of the food industry on the composition, food value, and suitability of foods for different groups of people

## Careers in the food industry

As the food industry is so large, there are a variety of avenues to explore if you are considering a career in it. Each of the groups listed on the previous page offer opportunities at different levels of qualification. It is perhaps best to decide first which main group you are interested in, then investigate it thoroughly to make sure it is suitable and worth pursuing for you.

You can find out about the qualifications and training you would need from a variety of sources:

the school careers advisor

local careers advice centre or job centre

by direct communication with a company, local council, food association, local health authority, etc. (find addresses and telephone numbers in the telephone directory)

by direct communicaton with colleges of further education, polytechnics or universities

It is often worth asking if you could visit and talk to someone who actually works in the sort of job you are interested in. You can then discuss all aspects of the job with someone who has first hand experience and information. Some schools offer vocational training with local industry and commerce during the school year.

## ▷ Things to do

1 Refer back to the groups of people involved in the food industry on page 5. Why is the job of the food and health inspector in each group especially important?
2 Make a list of the local companies in your area that are directly concerned with supplying the food industry with its requirements – e.g. packaging factories, feed suppliers, poultry farms, etc.
3 Why are we able to buy such a variety of foods (fresh as well as processed) from countries abroad?
4 How has computer technology helped the food retail industry to be more efficient? (Use the pictures below to help you.)

5 How have plastics revolutionized (changed) the food industry? Give examples in your answer.
6 What might be the advantages and disadvantages of the following jobs?
   Waiter/waitress in a restaurant that opens mainly in the evening
   checkout operator in a large food supermarket
   farm labourer
   production line worker in a sweets factory
   laboratory worker, checking milk samples for safety and hygiene
7 What might be the personal qualities required by someone with each of the following jobs?
   restaurant waiter/waitress
   checkout operator in a large food supermarket
   health inspector who visits shops and restaurants
   milk delivery person
   food technologist
   dietician working in a large hospital ◁

# Food investigations

## Why investigate food?

You may think you are reasonably capable of preparing and cooking food.

But how much do you know and understand about food and its composition, nutritional value, reaction with other ingredients etc.?

Food investigations provide you with knowledge about food and equip you with the information you need to make choices about your food intake.

## How to investigate food

There are numerous ways of investigating foods.

Some involve **objective** methods, where facts and figures are obtained by testing or measuring some aspect of the food, e.g. measuring a particular nutrient, or counting the number of people who buy a certain food in a survey.

Some involve **subjective** methods, where scores are obtained for a particular aspect of a food (e.g. flavour), based on the opinions of people who observe, taste, or smell the food.

It may be useful to test a food in more than one way in order to gain more information about it, e.g. when reducing the sugar content of a cake mixture, the volume of the cooked cakes could be measured and they could be tasted as the sugar content is reduced.

Whatever the chosen method for investigating a food, there are certain points to remember:

**1** Similar foods vary in their composition, depending on where they were grown or produced, and how long ago they were harvested. It may be necessary, therefore, to test more than one sample.

2 Weigh, measure, and record results and observations accurately.
3 Pay careful attention to hygiene and safety, especially if the food being investigated becomes unfit for consumption.
4 People who take part in tasting panels should be instructed carefully about how to give scores for food and should have no prior knowledge about how the food was prepared.

**Recording results and information**

The information you obtain from an investigation should be recorded and presented in such a way that it can be understood and used by others who read it. Lively illustrations, photographs, eyecatching captions, and clear explanations all help to get the information across. Some examples of ways of presenting information are given below.

Popularity of breakfast cereals

Total survey – 24 people

| Cereals | Oaty crunch | Wheat crispies | Rice pops | Others |
|---|---|---|---|---|
| Number of people | 10 | 6 | 5 | 3 |

Too much sugar used.

Healthy eating symbols used in a Supermarket.

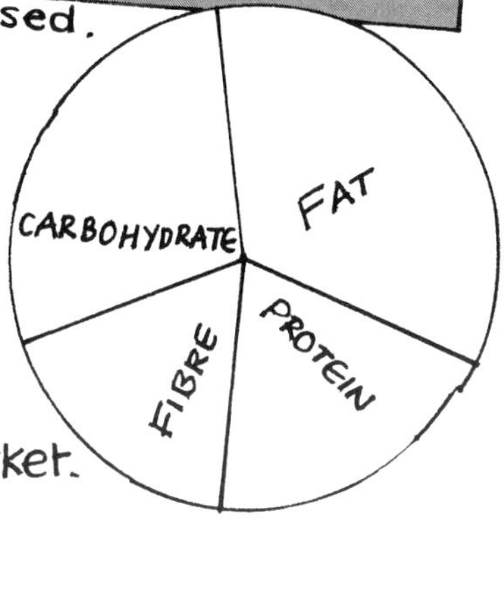

# Where does food come from?

The most obvious answer to this question is the supermarket. However, to understand more about food, you need to investigate its origins in more detail.

Have you ever considered that if it wasn't for the sun, you would be unable to eat a beefburger (or any other food for that matter)? To explain this, you need to study how plants and animals rely on each other for food. This is sometimes called the **food chain**, and is shown below in a simplified version – it is in fact much more detailed, with thousands of chemical reactions to make it work.

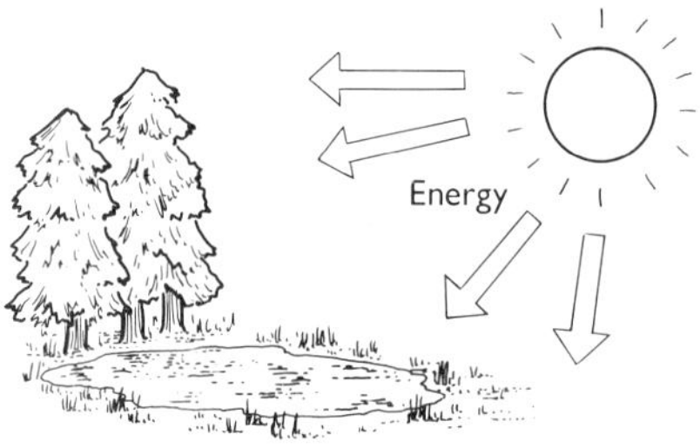


1 The sun emits (gives out) **energy**. This travels to the earth and is absorbed by **chlorophyll** in all green plants (from the smallest algae to the largest tree).

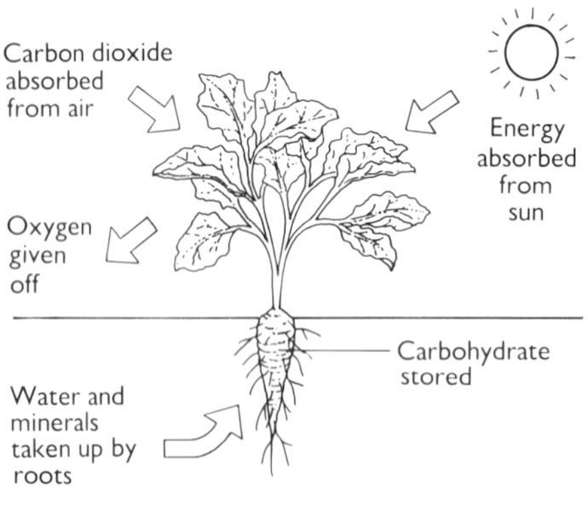


2 Plants make **carbohydrate** which they store. This process is called **photosynthesis**. Plants also make proteins and other substances, and to do this they need a supply of nutrients, water, warmth, and a suitable ground in which to grow.

3 Some animals eat plants only. They are called **herbivores**. People who eat only plant foods are called **vegans**. They are **herbivorous**.

4 Some animals eat plants and animals. They are called **omnivores**. Many people are **omnivorous**.

5 Some animals eat other animals only. This includes animal products such as eggs, milk, and blood. They are called **carnivores**. **Carnivorous** people are rare!

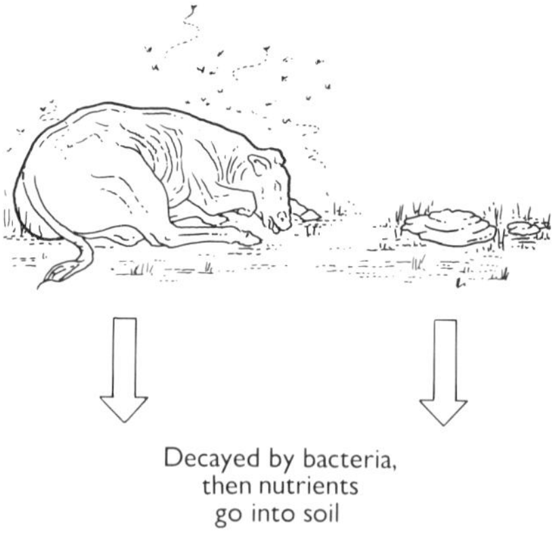


6 Animals (including people) excrete waste products, and dead plants and animals decay. This **fertilizes** (see page 13) the soil so that more plants grow.

So, without the sun, there would be no plants to feed cattle. Therefore there would be no beef and no beefburgers!

Most animals in the food chain cannot do anything to change the amount or type of food that they have. However, people can and do alter the food chain to suit themselves, and have been doing so for a long time. The effects of altering the food chain can have bad consequences for other animals and plants.

> Below is a list of the ways in which people have changed the food chain to suit themselves. For each one, find out how it has affected plants and animals and give an example: ◁

1 Cutting down large areas of trees, to plant vast areas of crops. Destroying hedgerows and jungles, etc.

2 Spraying crops with pesticides, insecticides, and herbicides. This destroys animals (e.g. insects) which eat the crops and plants which compete with plant crops for space, light and nutrients.

3 Using synthetic fertilizers (see page 13) in large quantities to grow crops in quick succession.

4 Domesticating and breeding animals in large numbers for use as food.

5 Catching large numbers of fish.

6 Disposing of waste products, e.g. sewage, chemicals, and rubbish, into the sea and on land.

7 Destroying the **ozone layer** above the earth with chemicals from aerosols, etc.

# Food production

The twentieth century has seen large increases in the amount of food grown by farmers, for the rest of the population to eat. In the centuries before, food production was on a much smaller scale. Many people lived in rural areas and produced their own food – they were **self-sufficient**. The main reasons for the increase in food production include:

1. More people rely on food being grown for them.
2. There are more people in the world to feed.
3. Many people can afford to buy more food.
4. More food is grown for preservation and processing.
5. In some countries, farmers are given incentives (usually grants of money or guaranteed prices for their crops) to grow certain types and quantities of food.

In Britain, farmers produce 65 per cent of all the food eaten. The rest is imported.

▷ Study the graphs below carefully. For each of the nine foods listed, write down which of the following points applies to them:

**Ways in which an increase in food production has been achieved**

1. Mechanization – development and greater use of large machines to plough, sow, spray, and harvest crops.
2. Better harvesting methods – less wastage.
3. Greater use of chemicals and medicines to control pests, diseases, weeds, etc.
4. Better soil fertility to grow crops (see opposite page).
5. Development of plants that produce higher yields.
6. Cross breeding of animals to produce larger and sturdier offspring.
7. Intensive breeding and rearing of livestock in large buildings under controlled conditions.

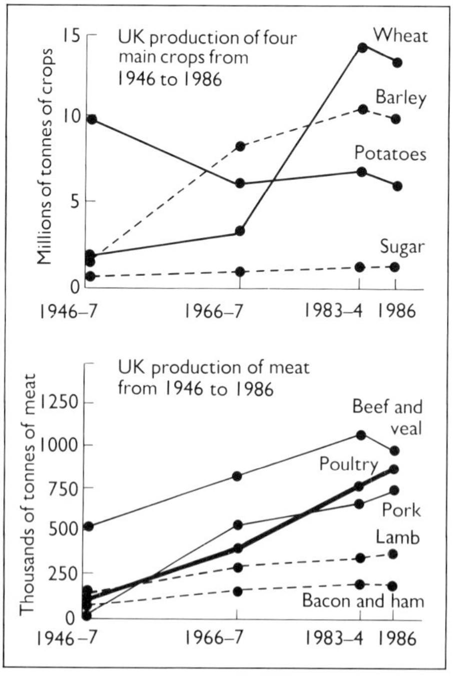


For example, if you think that 1, 2, and 4 apply to wheat, then write: 'Wheat production has increased due to mechanization, better harvesting methods and better soil fertility'. ◁

# Growing plant crops

When farmers want to grow a large quantity of plants, e.g. cereals, they have to make sure that they are provided with nutrients (see page 10). This is done by **fertilizing** the soil.

Fertilizers are applied to soil to provide plants with a variety of nutrients. There are two main groups of fertilizers:

1 chemically produced fertilizers (synthetic fertilizers)

2 organic fertilizers.

## Synthetic fertilizers

Most synthetic fertilizers contain **nitrogen** (N), **phosphorus** (P), and **potassium** (K). All of these are required for normal growth in plants. Nitrogen is especially important as it enables plants to make **proteins**. It also encourages fast growth, which is necessary if the farmer wants to use the same piece of land for two crops in a year.

## Organic fertilizers

The word 'organic' means that a substance contains the element **carbon** (C). Organic fertilizers include **manure** (animal excreta), **compost** (decayed plant matter), and **crop wastes** (e.g. cereal straw). These contain a variety of plant nutrients, some of which contain carbon. Organic fertilizers are often used in **mixed farming systems**. This is where crops, e.g. barley, are grown to feed animals reared for meat or dairy produce. Then the manure is put back on the land to grow more crops.

## What happens when fertilizers are added to the soil?

Not all the nutrients in fertilizers applied to soil are taken up by plants. Some nitrogen, in particular, is lost to the air as **ammonia**, or is **leached** (drained) through the soil as **nitrate**, because it is very soluble in water. This can happen with both synthetic and organic fertilizers. Some people have expressed concern about possible hazards to health, as the nitrogen can eventually end up in drinking water. Research is continuing into this problem, and as yet there is no firm evidence of a health hazard.

## Organic foods

Many health food shops and some supermarket chains now sell 'organic' foods. As all foods contain carbon, strictly speaking they are all organic. What the manufacturers mean is that the food with 'organic' on the label has been grown using organic fertilizers, and has usually had no pesticides (chemicals which kill insects etc., see page 11) or other chemicals applied to it. Some people believe that this is better for health, and is better for the **environment** (the land, air, water etc.). In the case of animal produce (meat and dairy foods), 'organic' would mean without using hormones to promote growth or antibiotics to prevent disease.

▷ Below are photographs showing some organically grown vegetables (top) compared with non-organically grown ones. Comment on their appearance, size, etc. ◁

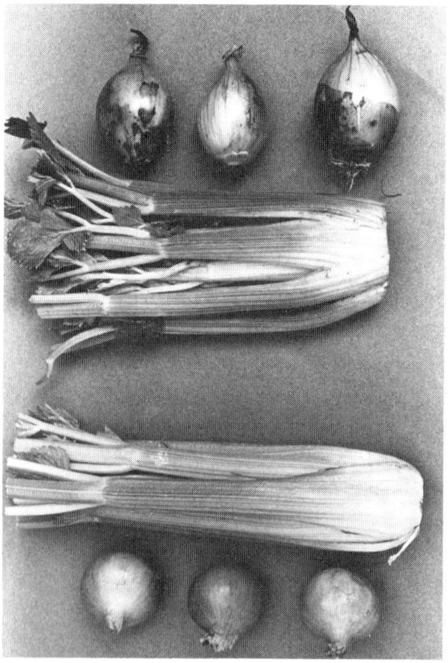

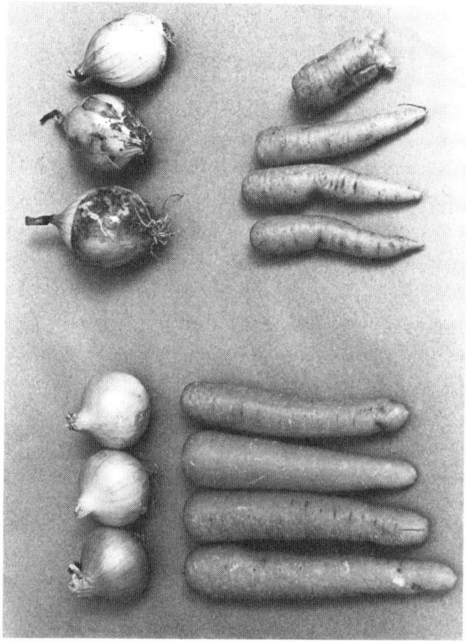

▷ Conduct a price survey of a variety of organic foods, compared with non-organic equivalents. You could include fruit and vegetables, dairy produce, canned and packet foods. If possible, visit a health food shop to survey the prices there. Comment on the prices, and on the way in which organic foods are presented to the consumer – e.g. what do they show on the labels, how are the foods described? ◁

▷ There are relatively few farmers who grow their food organically. What problems do you think they are likely to face if they produce their food in this way? ◁

▷ Find out what the Soil Association is, and how it helps farmers who wish to farm organically. ◁

# Food surpluses

Britain is a member of the European Economic Community (EEC). Agricultural production within the EEC is controlled by the Common Agricultural Policy (CAP). This policy aims to do the following:

1 increase agricultural production by the efficient use of technology and labour
2 give farmers a reasonable standard of living by guaranteeing the sale and price of certain commodities (foods they produce)
3 control imports of food from other countries to prevent competition
4 subsidize exports of food grown in the EEC to make them easier to sell in other countries
5 ensure that food supplies are available, when consumers want them, at a reasonable price

The CAP sets a **target price** for certain commodities. This is reviewed each year. Any commodities that cannot be sold at the target price are bought by the EEC at a slightly lower **intervention price**, and put into storage. Unless a commodity is limited by a **quota** (i.e. the farmer is only allowed to produce a certain amount), then farmers may produce as much as they like with a guaranteed sale.

The problem with this system is that it has led to large **surpluses** of food being stored. These surpluses are referred to as food mountains and lakes, and in 1986 they included:

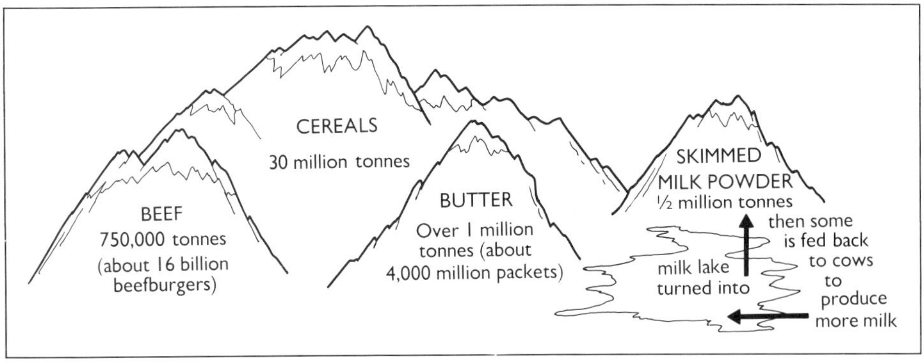


Fruit and vegetables that are surplus to requirement are often destroyed because storage is too difficult.

The whole issue of surpluses is the cause of much concern, argument, and dissatisfaction among politicians, farmers, and the public, especially as there are so many starving people in the world.

▷ Find out about the problems associated with sending food surpluses to countries where there is starvation on a large scale. What do you think about food surpluses? ◁

# What do plants need to grow?

All plants need nutrients and certain conditions in order to grow and multiply. **Yeast** is a microscopic, single celled plant, which is found naturally on the skins of fruits and in the air. **Cress** is a small, green leaved plant which grows quickly from seed. This investigation aims to find out the optimum (best) growing conditions for both of these plants.

## ▷ 1 Yeast investigation

You need:

dried yeast (*not* the type that is added directly to flour in bread making, called 'easy blend' yeast)
7 test tubes – large size
7 balloons
sugar and salt

*Method*

1 **Tube A (control)** One-third fill the tube with warm water (approximately 25–29°C). Carefully add half a level teaspoon of dried yeast and half a level teaspoon of sugar. Place a deflated balloon over the neck of the tube, and leave in a light warm place for half an hour. Observe and note what happens.
2 **Tube B** Repeat as for tube A, but leave in a **dark** warm place.
3 **Tube C** Repeat as for A, but **do not** add the sugar.
4 **Tube D** Repeat as for A, but use **cold** water, and leave in a cold place. Observe every half hour for 3–4 hours.
5 **Tube E** Repeat as for A, but add **salt** instead of sugar.
6 **Tube F** Repeat as for A, but use **boiling** water (*add very carefully*).
7 **Tube G** Leave out the water completely, and leave the yeast and sugar in a light warm place.

*Drawing conclusions*

1 Which tube had the largest balloon after half an hour? What caused the balloons to inflate?
2 Which tube gave the optimum conditions for the yeast to grow and multiply?
3 Explain why some balloons did not inflate.
4 What instructions should a recipe give to get the best results when using yeast to make bread?

## 2 Cress investigation

You need:

5 empty margarine tubs (oblong ones, 250 g size are suitable)
cotton wool and blotting paper
a packet of cress seeds (or mustard and cress)

*Method*

1 prepare each tub as follows:

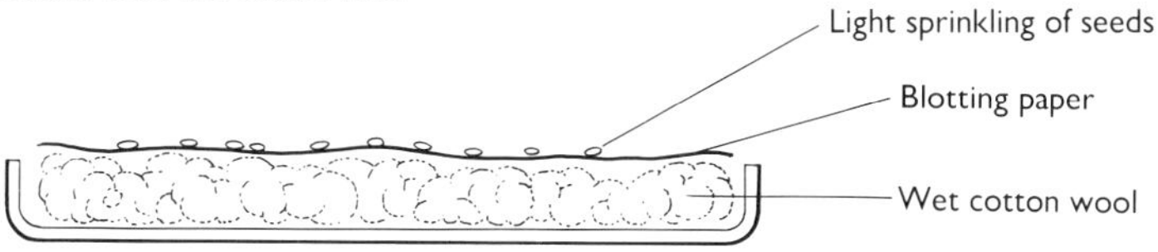


2 **Tub A (control)** Moisten the blotting paper and cotton wool with water. Sprinkle some seeds on to the paper (not too thickly). Leave in a light, fairly warm place – e.g. a kitchen windowsill. Keep moistened with water over the next few days. Observe how the seeds germinate and grow.
3 **Tub B** Repeat as for A, but place in a refrigerator.
4 **Tub C** Repeat as for A, but **do not** continue to water the seeds once the paper dries out.
5 **Tub D** Repeat as for A, but place the tub inside a box to **completely** eliminate light. Remember to water the seeds daily.
6 **Tub E** Repeat as for A, but place the tub inside a box to eliminate light, except for a small hole (made with a skewer) at one end of the lid. Remember to water the seeds daily.

*Drawing conclusions*

1 Notice and explain the difference in the appearances of the plants.
2 Which tub gave the optimum conditions for the cress to germinate and grow? Where does the cress seed obtain the materials it needs to germinate?
3 What are the similarities and differences between how yeast and cress plants grow (e.g. do they both need light)? ◁

## What do people need to grow and stay healthy?

▷ Look at the photographs below of diseases brought about by a deficiency (shortage) of nutrients. Find out the cause of each, and in which countries the disease most commonly occurs: ◁

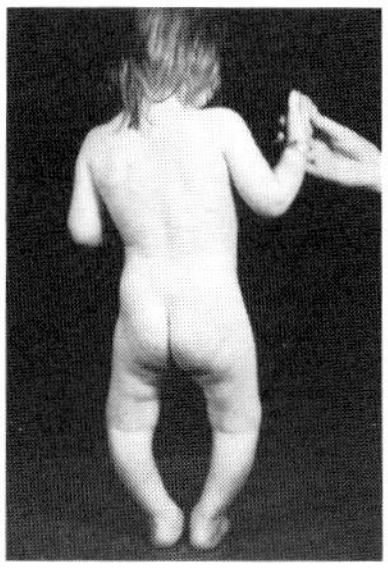
Rickets

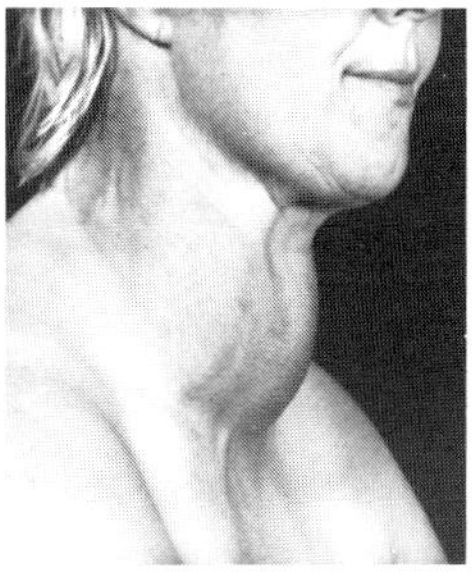
Goitre

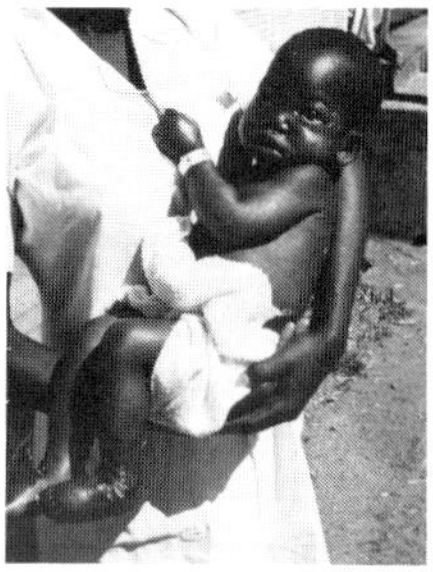
Kwashiorkor

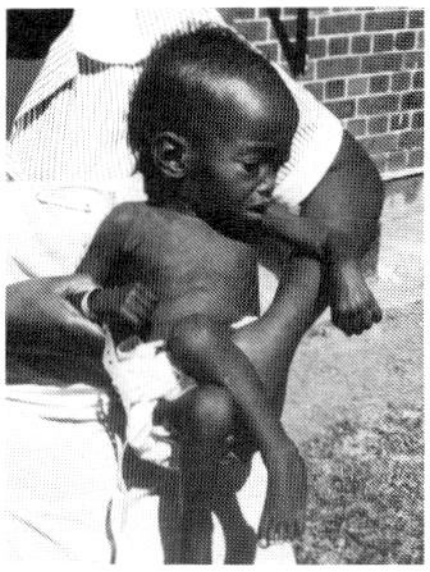
Marasmus

# Processing food

### Why are foods processed?

Most foods are processed in one or more ways before they are sold. There are several reasons why foods are processed, including:

1 to give a variety of products from a particular food, e.g. potatoes can be processed into frozen chips, oven chips, instant mashed potato, crisps, dried soups, potato salad, canned potatoes, etc.
2 to allow foods to be stored for a relatively long time, by preventing them from decaying, e.g. by freezing, pickling, canning, etc.
3 to provide a range of ready-to-eat or quick and easy-to-prepare foods (convenience foods)
4 to produce foods of a standard and uniform (same every time) quality so that consumers know what to expect from a certain product
5 to make foods **aesthetically appealing** (pleasing to look at, taste and smell).

### How are foods processed?

**Processing** means making a series of changes in something. In the case of food, processing can change a variety of things, e.g. colour, texture, keeping qualities, etc. It could mean a simple process of trimming the outer leaves off a cauliflower to make it more attractive and easy to see. It could also mean the more complex process of preparing and cooking the cauliflower as part of a complete frozen meal of cauliflower cheese.

> The chart opposite shows a list of processes applied to foods. Copy the list and complete the column of examples, by studying a variety of foods and finding out how they are processed. ◁

### > Things to do

Processed food to some people means food that has less food value than fresh food, because it has been 'messed about'. Some people feel that we eat too many processed foods in Britain. Prepare a short project, explaining what processing actually means, why it is necessary, and why processed foods are useful to most people.

Plan a day's meals, using your knowledge of nutrition (pages 22 and 23 will help), your imagination and skill, to include a variety of processed foods. Show how your chosen meals can meet the requirements of a healthy diet, and prepare the evening meal to illustrate this.

In your conclusion, explain how you think processed foods could be sensibly used in the daily intake of food, for a family of two adults and two children of school age. ◁

| Processing treatment | Reason | Examples |
|---|---|---|
| Ultra heat treatment | ⊗ ⋈ ⊙ | |
| Sterilization | ⊗ ⋈ | |
| Pasteurization | ⊗ ⋈ (some) | |
| Condensing | ↷ ✿ | |
| Evaporating | ↷ ○ | |
| Canning | ⊗ ⋈ ⊙ | |
| Pickling | ⊗ ⋈ ↷ | |
| Smoking/curing | ⊗ ⋈ ↷ | |
| Adding salt | ⊗ ⋈ ↷ | |
| Adding sugar | ⊗ ⋈ ↷ ✿ | |
| Freezing | ⊗ ⊙ | |
| Irradiation | ⊗ ⋈ ✿ | |
| Dehydrating | ⊗ ⋈ | |
| Freeze drying | ⊗ ⋈ | |
| Colouring | ✿ | |
| Adding flavouring | ✿ | |
| Emulsifying | ⦶ | |
| Stabilizing | ⦶ ✿ | |
| Milling | ↷ ⊙ ⊕ | |
| Refining | ↷ 🔍 ✿ | |
| Pre-cooking | ⊙ ✿ | |
| Pre-peeling/slicing/chopping | ⊙ ✿ | |
| Adding raising agent | ↷ ⊙ | |
| Hydrogenating | ↷ | |

The processes listed here are those most commonly used.

**Key to symbols**

- ⊗ prevents growth of microrganisms
- ⋈ destroys microrganisms present in food
- ↷ changes the food into a different product
- 🔍 removes impurities from food
- ⊙ convenience
- ⦶ prevents food from separating
- ⊕ breaks food down, so parts of it can be extracted
- ✿ makes food aesthetically pleasing

# Nutrition labels

At present, most food products have to show certain information on the label, e.g. ingredients, sell-by or best before date, quantity, etc. Food labelling laws are enforced to help consumers make informed choices when buying food, and to protect them from incorrect or misleading information. New regulations are to be introduced to cover nutrition labels. Many manufacturers already give information about the nutritional value of their product, which is of value to consumers. The new regulations will require the **total fat content** of most foods to be stated on the label, along with the maximum **saturated fatty acid content** of the fat (see page 33). In addition, new guidelines are being prepared to cover the way in which nutrition information is presented on labels. This is to help to prevent confusion because at present, nutrition information is given in a variety of different ways, which makes it hard for consumers to interpret what is in their food. Some examples of commonly used nutrition labels are given below:

A

**100 g of this product contains:**

250 kcal / 1040 kJ
2.5 g fat
13.0 g protein
46.0 g carbohydrate
27 g fibre

B

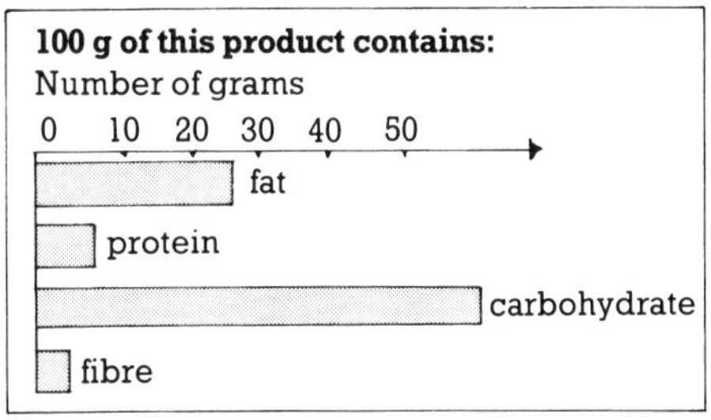


C

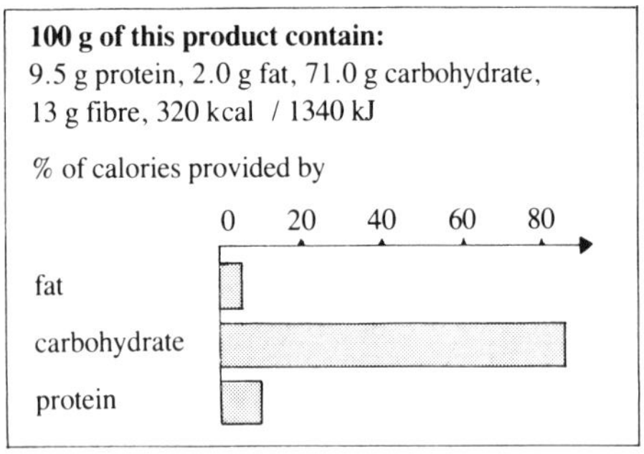


To be of any real value, nutrition labels should enable people to:

1 work out easily how much of a particular nutrient there is in a serving of the food.
2 compare how much of one nutrient there is with other nutrients in the same food.
3 compare the nutrient content of one food with another food.

▷ **Investigation: How much do people understand about the information given on nutrition labels?**
(This could be carried out as a group survey.)

Surveys conducted by the Consumers' Association, Ministry of Agriculture Fisheries and Food, and the National Consumer Council suggest that the way in which nutrition information is presented on food labels does cause confusion and in some cases is hard to interpret. Put this to the test by carrying out your own survey, as follows.

Study the nutrition labels on the opposite page, then ask as many people as possible the following:

**1** Which food contains the most **a** fat, **b** protein?

**2** Which food contains the least **a** carbohydrate, **b** fibre?

The correct answers are given at the foot of the page. Work out from which labels the correct answers were given most frequently and least frequently. Comment on your findings. ◁

▷ Surveys have also concluded that to be effective, nutrition labels need to be clearly worded and not too technical. With this in mind, design your own nutrition label for a specific food (use food tables to provide the information you require). You could do another survey with this and other people's labels, to test their effectiveness. ◁

▷ Nutrition labels often give the amount of nutrients **per 100 g** of the food, which may be difficult to visualize. The two activities below are designed to help you interpret the nutritional information, and could be included in the group survey above:

**1** Study the label below, which is from a packet of wholewheat crisps, weighing 25 g. How much of the following nutrients would you get, if you ate all of the crisps in the packet?
**a** protein, **b** fat, **c** carbohydrate, **d** fibre (answers at foot of page)

**Typical nutritional content per 100 g**
Protein 10 g    Carbohydrate 12 g
Fat 30 g    Fibre 18 g

**2** Collect the nutrition labels from the following three foods: wholemeal sliced bread, soft margarine, and cheddar cheese. Work out how much fibre, fat, and carbohydrate you would get from a cheese sandwich made with the following amounts: 75 g bread, 15 g margarine, and 40 g cheese. Use the information on label C opposite. The example below will help you:

| | | |
|---|---|---|
| 75 g food contains: | fibre | – 75% of 13 g = 9.75 g |
| | fat | – 75% of 2 g = 1.5 g |
| | carbohydrate | – 75% of 71 g = 53.25 g ◁ |

▷ Collect some labels to show how some of the supermarket companies are trying to make nutrition labelling easier to understand and use. ◁

**Answers to questions**
1a B b A
2a A b B

1 protein = 2.5 g
fat = 7.5 g
carbohydrate = 3 g
fibre = 4.5 g

# The nutritional value of processed food

Processing makes a series of changes in food, and in some cases this may also mean a change in the nutritional value. Such changes include the following:

## Damage to nutrients

Some nutrients are susceptible to damage during heating:

**Vitamin C** (ascorbic acid) is easily **oxidized** (it combines with oxygen), and if this process goes too far, vitamin C cannot be used by the body.

**Vitamin $B_1$** (thiamin) is destroyed by heat, so is some **vitamin $B_2$** (riboflavin).

**Protein** molecules are **denatured** (changed) by heat, and if overheated, the protein becomes less valuable to the body.

## Loss of nutrients

Some nutrients are soluble in water, and can therefore be easily lost. These include vitamin C, vitamin $B_1$, vitamin $B_6$, vitamin $B_{12}$, and nicotinic acid (one of the B vitamins).

Some nutrients are lost when a food is refined:

**Vitamin $B_1$** (thiamin) is lost during rice milling, as it is concentrated in the outer layers of the rice grain, which are removed. If the rice is parboiled before milling, then some of the vitamin will pass into the middle of the grain and so will not be lost. Easy-cook rice is parboiled.

**Dietary fibre** (not strictly a nutrient, but nevertheless important) is lost when cereal grains are milled, as it is found on the outside of the grains.

## Gain of nutrients

Some foods gain other nutrients when they are processed, some of which may not be always desirable:

**Fat** is absorbed by some foods such as potatoes, when they are fried.

**Sugar** is added to fruits to preserve them as jam or canned fruit.

## Does it matter if nutrients are lost during processing?

If people eat a good variety of foods including fresh, unprocessed foods, then the losses of nutrients in some processed foods are likely to be made up by other foods. Problems arise where food is limited, e.g. in countries where the consumption of refined (polished) rice is high, as in the Far East. People there may develop **beri-beri**, which is a deficiency of vitamin $B_1$.

# Food manufacturers and nutrition

Food manufacturers are generally keen to promote the health-giving features of the foods they sell. Where the nutritional value of a food has been changed by processing, the manufacturer can take steps to minimize the changes. This can be done in the following ways:

1. By **restoring** the nutrient content to that originally present in the food before it was processed, e.g. white flour often has vitamins added before being made into bread.
2. By **enriching** the food, which means adding more of a nutrient than is normally present in the food, e.g. fruit juices often have extra vitamin C added.
3. By **fortification**, which means adding nutrients not normally present in a food, e.g. vitamins A and D are added to margarine by law, as it is often used as a substitute for butter which naturally contains those vitamins.

Many manufacturers have produced foods in response to the requirements of the NACNE and COMA dietary goal recommendations. It is easy to buy low fat, low sugar, and high fibre versions of familiar products such as milk, cheese, cream, jam, breakfast cereals, and biscuits. Consumers need to be selective, as some of these products may draw attention to a particular goal, e.g. high fibre, but may also have a high fat or sugar content. There are certain requirements for labelling foods that have to be followed, before manufacturers can make certain claims about their products, i.e.:

| | |
|---|---|
| Low fat foods | – must not contain more than 50% of the fat content normally found in the product. |
| Low sugar foods | – must not contain more than 50% of the sugar content (all sugars – see page 34) normally found in the product. |
| High fibre foods | – one serving of the product must contain at least 4.2 g of fibre. |
| Low salt foods | – must not contain more than 50% of the salt content normally found in the product. |
| Low calorie foods | – neither 100 g nor a serving of the product (whichever is larger) should provide more than 167 kJ (40 kcal). |

▷ Make a survey of which groups of food products actively promote the vitamin and mineral content on the food label. Do the same for the fat content, energy value, and sugar content of a variety of products. How well do the products in your survey meet all the dietary goals? ◁

▷ Which processing treatments (refer back to page 19) are likely to lead to the greatest changes in the nutritional value of the foods that are processed in that way? ◁

# Food additives

Foods often have extra substances added to them during processing. These substances are called **food additives**. Some people call these 'chemicals', and object to having them put into their food. However, **all** substances (including the food itself) consist of chemicals, so it is important to find out and understand what food additives are and why they are used.

The reasons why additives are used include:

**1** to prevent food from decaying (going 'off')
**2** to produce food of a reliable and standard quality
**3** to enhance (help the development and intensity of) the flavour, colour, texture, and appearance of food
**4** to assist the processing of food
**5** to improve or maintain the nutritional value of food.

Food manufacturers are allowed by law to use only certain additives. These have been passed as safe for consumption by food safety committees, as a result of extensive tests and trials.

Some food additives are made in a science laboratory (**synthetic** additives) from pure chemicals. Some additives are extracted from plants or animals (**natural** additives). It is easier to control the purity of synthetic additives than natural ones.

Food additives are listed on food labels, and most appear as EEC code numbers.

Sometimes the full chemical names of additives are given, as in the example here.

> Contains polypropylene glycol alginate, polysorbate 60 and sorbitan monostearate

| EEC code number | What they are/what they do | Examples (N = natural, S = synthetic) |
|---|---|---|
| 100–199 | Food colours | E100 curcumin (N)<br>E110 sunset yellow (S) |
| 200–283 | Mainly preservatives<br>Some acids (bring out flavour) | E270 lactic acid (N)<br>223 sodium metabisulphite (S) |
| 300–341 | mainly antioxidants (stop foods containing fat from going off) | E306 tocopherol (N)<br>E321 butylated hydroxytoluene (S) |
| 400 onwards | emulsifiers (see pages 50–51), stabilizers, thickeners, etc. (to mix foods or stop them from separating) | E406 agar (N)<br>E466 carboxymethylcellulose (S) |

There are a variety of reasons why some people object to the use of additives in food. These include the following:

1 Some additives may have adverse (bad) effects on people who are sensitive to them.
2 Even though additives are tested before being used in food, it may not be possible to predict what the long term effects of eating them are.
3 Some additives may be used to mask inferior ingredients used in convenience foods.
4 Some are unnecessary (e.g. colours and flavours), as they mask the natural qualities of food.

## Additives on food labels

Food manufacturers are obliged to state any food additives they have used on the ingredients list. An additive is usually listed under a category name, e.g. preservatives, antioxidants, colours, to explain what function it performs in the food.

With the demand for more natural foods, many manufacturers make a point of emphasizing which additives they do *not* put into the food, e.g.

This does not necessarily mean that the food does not contain *any* additives. A consumer would need to examine the food label to establish whether the product did contain other categories of additive.

▷ As a group survey, each study the labels of five food products which state that the food does not contain artificial additives, or is free from preservatives, colours, flavourings, or sugar. Check the ingredients list carefully, and note any other additives that are included – a list of E numbers will be useful to help you. Add together the total number of products in your survey which do contain other additives. Comment on this, and the effect that labels such as 'Free from artificial additives' or 'No preservatives' have on your first impressions of the product.

Ask a group of people (e.g. shoppers at a local store) if they are influenced by such labels when they are choosing their food.

Based on your findings, prepare a short project about food additives, making sure that you present the arguments both for and against their use in foods. How would you advise consumers when choosing their food, so that they have an informed view about additives? ◁

## ▷ Investigation: Food colours

This particular group of food additives has attracted much publicity, as it is known that certain colourings can cause adverse effects in some children. Colourings are widely used to make food more appealing to consumers. However, manufacturers are increasingly using colours extracted from plants to make their products more natural.

**1 Does the colour of strawberry milkshake influence our perception of flavour?**

You need:

575 ml (1 pint) cool milk
1 small can strawberries in light syrup
a few drops pink food colouring
a liquidizer
a strainer and bowl
2 jugs, labelled A and B
glasses for sampling

*Method*

1 Place the milk and strawberries in the liquidizer. Run it for a few seconds until the mixture is smooth.
2 Pour the mixture through the strainer into the bowl.
3 Divide the mixture equally between the two jugs.
4 Add the pink colouring **a drop at a time** to the contents of jug A, until they have a noticeably pinker colour than the contents of jug B.
5 Pour the milkshake from each jug into glasses (e.g. 10 from each jug).
6 Ask a group of people (who must not know anything about the investigation) to look at and taste a glass of milkshake from each.
7 Then ask them to complete a copy of the chart below:

| **Milkshake** | **Appearance rating 1–5** (1 = least liked, 5 = most liked) | **Flavour rating 1–5** (1 = least fruity, 5 = most fruity) |
|---|---|---|
| A | | |
| B | | |

*Drawing conclusions*

1 Work out which milkshake was most liked in appearance, as follows: Add up all the numbers for appearance for milkshake A, then for B. The milkshake with the highest score will have been most liked, and the one with the lowest score will have been least liked. If the scores are the same or very near, then most people will have found little difference.
2 Work out which milkshake was most liked for flavour in the same way.
3 Did the addition of the pink food colouring seem to have any influence on people's perception of flavour?
4 Why would a food manufacturer find this sort of information useful when developing a product?
5 What is meant by **market research**? Have you ever taken part in any market research?

**2 How yellow does custard need to be?**

You need:

150 ml (¼ pint) milk
1 rounded dessertspoon cornflour
1 egg yolk
12.5 g (½ oz) sugar
a few drops vanilla flavouring
½ can ready made custard
small packet instant custard, made as directed on packet

150 ml (¼ pint) milk
1 rounded dessertspoon custard powder (several brands could be compared) plus sugar to taste
Note: keep the ingredients labels from each packet.

*Method*

1 Prepare the first custard (labelled A). Put the cornflour into a pan, and gradually blend in the milk with a wooden spoon. Add the sugar. Heat, stirring all the time, until it thickens and boils. Remove from the heat, cool for 2–3 minutes. Stir in the egg yolk and vanilla flavouring. Pour the custard into a (heatproof) glass dish.
2 Prepare the second custard (labelled B). Put the custard powder into a pan, and gradually blend in the milk. Add the sugar. Heat, stirring all the time, until it thickens and boils. Pour the custard into a (heatproof) glass dish. If any other brands are made, label them C, D, etc.
3 Pour the made up instant custard into a glass dish,and label it.
4 Warm the ready made custard in a pan – be careful not to boil it, as this spoils the flavour. Pour it into a glass dish and label it.
5 Ask a group of people (who must not know anything about the investigation), e.g. 10, to look at each custard in turn, taste them and complete the chart below:

| Custard | Colour rating 1–5 (1 = palest yellow, 5 = brightest yellow) | Flavour rating 1–5 (1 = least liked, 5 = most liked) |
|---|---|---|
| A<br>B<br>etc. | | |

*Drawing conclusions*

1 Work out which custard was most and least liked for flavour, and rated the palest and brightest yellow, in the same way as for the milkshakes.
2 Did the colour of the custards seem to have any influence on whether or not people liked the flavour?
3 Did any of the commercial custards contain food colourings? If so, were they natural or synthetic colourings?
4 What is the advantage in using egg yolk to colour home made custard?
5 From your investigation, do you think there is any need to colour custard?
6 How might this information be useful to the parents of a hyperactive child? ◁

# Water in food

Some foods have a naturally high water content, e.g. fruits, vegetables, milk, meat, and eggs.

Some processed foods have water added to them during processing, e.g. as a syrup for canned fruit, as brine for canned fish, as an ice glaze for frozen seafood, or as part of a recipe such as soup.

As water is quite heavy, its addition to processed foods may increase their price, particularly if the food is sold by weight. Water does not supply the body with energy, so it is used in a variety of foods which are sold as low calorie or reduced fat. In this way, the water adds either bulk or moisture to the food, particularly in reduced fat foods.

## ▷ Investigation: The use of water in reduced fat foods

You need:
50 g (2 oz) margarine
50 g (2 oz) low fat spread
2 small pans
2 glass graduated measuring cylinders and funnels

*Method*

1 Melt the margarine and low fat spread in separate pans, gently, and observe and note what happens as they melt.
2 When they are completely melted, carefully pour each liquid into a separate measuring cylinder, and allow them to settle. Note the quantity of liquid in each.

*Drawing conclusions*

1 What was different about the way in which each fat melted?
2 Explain the amounts of liquid in each cylinder.
3 Why is low fat spread unsuitable for use in pastries and for frying?
4 Why are emulsifiers added to low fat spreads?
5 Study the nutritional informaton on a pack of low fat spread. How does it compare with ordinary margarine for energy value and fat content? Comment on the value of low fat spreads in slimming diets. ◁

## ▷ Investigation: Comparison of dried and canned food products

You need:
a variety of dried foods (see below) and their canned or carton equivalents, e.g. apricots, prunes, lentils, kidney beans, butter beans, soups, skimmed milk
Note: make a note of the price and weight of each packet and can or carton used in this investigation, which should be on the packet or label.

*Method*

1 Open each can or carton and tip the contents into a dish or measuring jug, with a label showing the weight and price of the product.
2 For beans, fruit etc. in a syrup or other liquid, strain off the liquid and then weigh the solid food separately, and keep a note of the weights.
3 Count out the same number of dried beans or fruits that were in each can, weigh them, and soak these overnight in water. Weigh them after soaking. Keep a note of the weights.
4 Cook each dried food by boiling them in water, until they are tender and ready to eat. Make a note of how long they take to cook and their weight. Note: For dried soups and milk, make up the same **volume** as the canned equivalent, and make a note of how long they take to prepare and cook (if required).
5 Work out the cost of each dried food and its canned equivalent in the following way:

Chick peas

**canned**
35p for 200 g (after liquid strained off)

$\therefore \quad 1\,\text{g} = \frac{35}{200} = 0.175\text{p}$

$\therefore \quad 100\,\text{g} = 17.5\text{p}$

**dried**
60p for 400 g (dried)
60p for 1200 g (cooked)

$\therefore \quad 1\,\text{g} = \frac{60}{1200} = 0.05\text{p}$

$\therefore \quad 100\,\text{g} = 5\text{p}$ (plus a little more for cooking)

6 Taste the cooked results for both canned and dried foods.

*Drawing conclusions*

1 Were there any noticeable price differences between the canned and dried foods? Comment on your findings.
2 Could the liquid in the canned foods (not applicable to soups or milk) be used in any useful way?
3 How do dried foods absorb water when they are soaked?
4 Comment on the difference in preparation and cooking between the canned and dried foods. How would this influence your choice of canned or dried foods?
5 Comment on the texture and flavour of the cooked foods (compare dried with canned foods).
6 Why is the packaging for dried foods usually less expensive than for canned foods? What other factors influence the cost of these foods, apart from packaging? ◁

# Food and health

Have you ever eaten anything that made you ill a short time afterwards, or maybe the next day? The chances are that the food you chose to eat was **bad** ('off') in some way, but you didn't know.

It is difficult to imagine that if you make bad (unwise) choices of food when you are young, you may become ill as a result, in 20, 30 or 40 years' time.

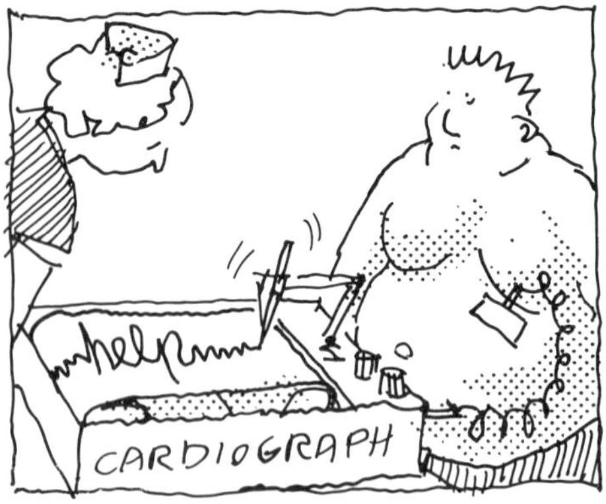


However, research carried out in recent years has revealed that there is a link between some of the common illnesses such as heart disease and intestinal disorders, and the types and amounts of food which people have eaten in the past.

Preparing, cooking,and eating food should be a satisfying and enjoyable experience. Choosing a healthy diet doesn't have to be boring, especially as most people in Britain have plenty to choose from.

There are guidelines to help people choose a healthy diet. We have the responsibility of looking after our own health, so it is for us to decide how far to follow dietary advice.

It is more interesting and healthier to choose a **mixture** of fresh and processed foods each day. This gives your body a greater variety of nutrients to use. Try to limit the number of foods that contain large amounts of fat, sugar, and salt. Food labels often give you information about this.

# Fat in food – what do you need to know?

Dietary guidelines suggest that we should reduce the amount of fat that we eat to 30 per cent of our **energy** intake.

Energy is needed by the body for all its processes and functions. Energy is released from food after it has been digested and absorbed, by a process called **oxidation**. Fat supplies more than **twice** the amount of energy as the same amount of protein or carbohydrate.

If the amount of food someone eats supplies more energy than they need, the excess energy is stored in fatty (adipose) tissue under the skin. If this process continues, then gradually that person's weight will increase. It is important, therefore, to try and get the energy balance right, so that:

## Which foods contain fat?

Many foods contain relatively large amounts of fat, which is not obvious at first glance. This is called 'invisible' or 'hidden' fat. The energy value of such foods will therefore be high.

Some foods are virtually all fat, e.g. butter, margarine, lard, and suet.

## ▷ Investigation: Do people know which foods contain fat?

If people want to alter their dietary intake of fat, they need to know which foods to avoid or cut down on. This investigation takes the form of a survey. Try to ask as many people as possible, of different age groups, and pool your results as a group.

Prepare a list of the following foods, clearly displayed on a piece of card or paper, for people to study. If possible, put a picture of each food by its name:

- chocolate ☐
- bread ☐
- cheddar cheese ☐
- meat pie ☐
- biscuits (sweet and savoury) ☐
- fruit cake ☐
- boiled potatoes ☐
- ice cream ☐
- natural low fat yogurt ☐
- cottage cheese ☐
- chips ☐
- danish pastry ☐
- butter ☐
- sausages ☐
- crisps ☐
- salad cream ☐
- peanuts (roasted) ☐
- margarine ☐
- beefburgers ☐
- steamed plaice ☐

Give each person a piece of paper with this list printed on it, and give them the following information:

> You are trying to reduce your fat intake. Tick the foods in this list that you would need to eat less of. Then write down the names of five foods from the list that contain the least fat.

Then ask each person to read the following questions (also displayed on a piece of paper), and to write down the correct answer (1, 2, or 3) on their piece of paper:

**a saturated fats . . .**
**1** contain too much water
**2** in excess can be bad for the heart
**3** are only found in butter

**b cholesterol . . .**
**1** is a flavouring in margarine
**2** is another name for fat
**3** in excess amounts, speeds up the blocking of arteries

**c margarine . . .**
**1** gives the body more calories than butter
**2** gives the body fewer calories than butter
**3** gives the body the same amount of calories as butter

**d cooking oil . . .**
**1** has the same amount of fat as solid fat
**2** has less fat because it has water added
**3** gives the body less calories than solid fat

correct answers: **a 2, b 3, c 3, d 1**

*Drawing conclusions*

1 Add up the number of ticks for each food on the list, and present your results in a bar chart.
2 The five foods in the list with the least fat are bread, boiled potatoes, yogurt, steamed plaice, and cottage cheese. Add up the number of times these foods were given as a correct answer for foods with the least fat.
3 Apart from the five foods listed in 2 above, all the rest contain relatively large amounts of fat. Which food was most frequently ticked as ones to eat less of? Were any of the five low fat foods ticked? From your results, do the people in your survey seem aware of the fat content of foods?
4 For each of the four questions, add up the number of correct answers that were given in your survey. From your results, do the people questioned seem to understand the scientific words used about fat (saturated, cholesterol, etc.), and the similarities between margarine, butter and oils?
5 Present your results as a group display. Try to include clear messages in your display about fat content of foods, the meanings of words used on food labels, and ways that people can reduce their fat intake.

## What is fat?

There are a variety of words which you will come across in books, on food labels, etc., used in connection with the subject of fats. You will have a clearer understanding of fats if you know why the words are used. Some explanations are given below. For each one, list the book or food label where you have seen it used:

| Words | Meaning | |
|---|---|---|
| Fatty acids | The main part of a fat molecule. Made of carbon (C) and hydrogen (H) atoms, mainly linked together by **single bonds**   The whole molecule is called a **triglyceride** | |
| Saturated fatty acids or 'saturated fats' or saturates | These are full up with H atoms and cannot accept any more 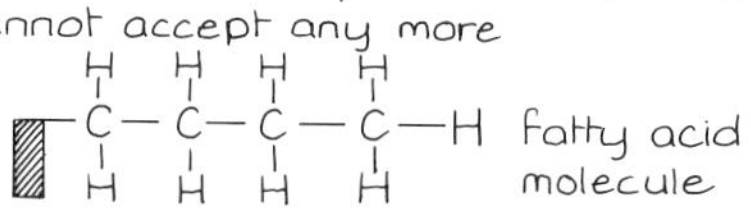  | Most fats are a **mixture** of these. Some fats have mostly polyunsaturated fatty acids. Some fats have mostly saturated fatty acids. |
| Unsaturated fatty acids or 'unsaturated' fats' | These have some of their C atoms linked by **double bonds** 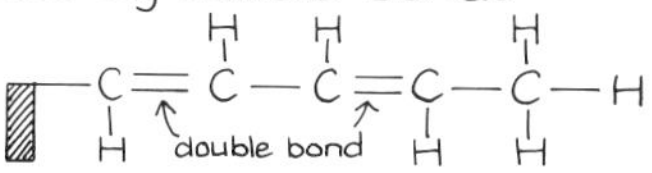  | |
| Polyunsaturated fatty acids or 'polyunsaturated fats' | These have **several** double bonds (poly means many) | |
| Monosaturated fatty acids | These have only **one** double bond | |
| Cis fatty acids, trans fatty acids | Double bonds cause the fatty acid molecules to **bend** (saturated ones are more or less straight). The more double bonds, the more bends there are. Cis and trans are the scientific terms used to describe the particular shape into which they bend. | |
| Hydrogenation or 'hydrogenated fats or oils' | Unsaturated fats can accept more H atoms, because the double bond breaks easily to make space for them. It is possible to pass hydrogen gas under controlled conditions through unsaturated oils. This makes them become saturated, and more solid. | |

Dietary guidelines also recommend that of the 30 per cent of energy we should have from fats, 20 per cent should come from unsaturated fats and only 10 per cent from saturated fats. This is because research has shown that eating too many saturated fats may be a factor leading to heart disease, so it is sensible to limit the amount you eat.

# Sugar in food – what do you need to know?

Do you eat a lot of sugar? The average person in Britain eats 38 kg (84 lb) of sucrose (ordinary sugar) per year. Dietary guidelines suggest that it would be better for our health to cut sugar intake by half.

## Sugar in food

Sucrose is one of a group of substances called **sugars**. All sugars provide the body with energy, but they provide little else. If eaten in excess, the energy released from the sugar in the body is stored as fat under the skin. This can lead to becoming overweight. Excess sugar can also make the teeth more vulnerable to **decay**.

It is useful to know the chemical names of the sugars, as these are often printed on food labels:

| Chemical name | Sometimes called |
|---|---|
| Sucrose | Sugar (caster, granulated, icing, brown) or invert sugar |
| Fructose | Fruit sugar |
| Lactose | Milk sugar |
| Maltose | Maltodextrin or malt |
| Glucose | Dextrose |

It is important to read food labels carefully if you are reducing your sugar intake. Sometimes a product will be labelled 'low sugar' or 'low sucrose', but may still contain some of the other sugars listed above. Some products, such as some meat sauces, peanut butter and savoury snacks may also contain sugar, though you might not expect them to. The higher on the ingredients list the sugar appears, the more there is in a food product. If nutritional information on the label gives a figure for **carbohydrate**, this will include sugars as well as starches, unless otherwise stated.

### ▷ Investigation: How often is sugar added to manufactured foods?

This will take the form of a group survey. Each person should read the ingredients list from five varieties of foods from the groups given below (or more if possible). Note how many of the foods contain any of the sugars listed above. Present your findings in the most appropriate way.

Groups of foods:
- dried or canned soups
- sauces
- canned vegetables
- fruit drinks
- canned and packet meat products
- baby foods
- pudding mixes
- jams and spreads
- breakfast cereals
- biscuits
- savoury snacks ◁

## ▷ Investigation: Are low sugar alternatives acceptable?

In response to dietary goal recommendations,some food manufacturers have produced low sugar alternatives to some of the foods they sell. They have either reduced the total amount of sugar in the product, or substituted the sugar with a sweetener, such as saccharin, aspartame etc., which do not give the body energy or lead to tooth decay.

Set up a taste panel, using some of the products listed below. Ask the people in your panel (who must not know which products you are testing) to taste each one in turn, and to rate its sweetness on a 1 to 5 scale (1 = least sweet, 5 = most sweet). Then ask them to state which one they most liked out of a group of similar products (e.g. which brand of baked beans they preferred).

Products to test (low sugar varieties and varieties sweetened with sugar or sweetener):

- baked beans in tomato sauce
- fruit yogurts
- fruit squashes and cordials
- jams and marmalades
- baby rusks
- instant pudding mixes

*Drawing conclusions*

1 Work out the percentage of savoury food products in your survey that contained sugar (of any type). Comment on your findings. Why do you think the sugar is added?

2 Were any of the sweetened products in your survey (such as breakfast cereals, savoury snacks) packaged and presented in a way that would appeal to children? Comment on your findings

3 From your taste panel, work out which food in each group of products tested was rated as the most sweet (highest score), and the least sweet (lowest score). How did these ratings compare with the food in each group that most people preferred (i.e. was the sweetest one most or least preferred)? Comment on your findings.

4 At what times of the day are you most likely to eat foods with a relatively high sugar content? Why do you eat them at these times? List the most likely ways that you could reduce **your** sugar intake. Do you think that you would benefit by eating less sugar?

5 What advice would you give to young parents about developing their baby's eating habits? What pressures might they come up against that might make them give the baby sweet foods at a very young age?

6 Investigate how food manufacturers try to cater for the needs and likes of diabetic people. ◁

## ▷ Investigation: How much sugar do you need to use in home-made recipes?

Many recipes for cakes, biscuits, puddings, etc. use sugar for sweetening, and in some cases as an important ingredient for trapping air or stabilizing a mixture. It is possible in many recipes to reduce the sugar content, or to use alternative ingredients (such as dried fruit) to sweeten the mixture, without adversely affecting the result. If you are reducing your sugar intake, you could try experimenting by reducing the amount you use. The recipe for biscuits below is one experiment – you may like to try others.

You need:

| | |
|---|---|
| **Mixture 1 (control)** | 175 g (6 oz) plain flour, 75 g (3 oz) margarine, 75 g (3 oz) caster sugar, 1 egg (size 5) |
| **Mixture 2** | As for mixture 1, but use only 50 g (2 oz) caster sugar |
| **Mixture 3** | As for mixture 1, but use only 25 g (1 oz) caster sugar |

*Method (same for each mixture)*

**1** Cream the margarine and sugar until light and fluffy.
**2** Add the egg gradually.
**3** Stir in the sieved flour to form a fairly stiff dough. Knead until smooth on a floured surface.
**4** Roll out to 6 mm (¼″) thick, cut out and place on a greased baking tray.
**5** Bake at gas 4, 180 °C (350 °F) for 15–20 minutes until golden. Cool on a wire rack.
**6** Place the biscuits on a plate, labelled 1, 2, or 3, depending on which mixture they are made from.
**7** Ask 10 people to try a biscuit from each plate (they should not be told what each mixture contained), taking a drink of water in between each one to clear their taste buds.
**8** Ask them to write on a piece of paper a score for each biscuit, from 1 to 5 (1 = do not like, 5 = like very much). They should be instructed not to compare one biscuit with another, but to give a score for each biscuit on its own.
**9** Add up the scores for each biscuit mixture. Each has a maximum score of 50.

*Drawing conclusions*

**1** Present your results in a chart, showing the most and least liked mixture.
**2** From your results, were the biscuits with the reduced sugar content (mixtures 2 and 3) still acceptable to most of the people in your survey (i.e. did they score 30 or more each)?
**3** How could you use this information when preparing food for people who are trying to reduce their sugar intake?
**4** Did the reduced amount of sugar appear to have any effect on the finished appearance of the biscuits (compared with the control)? ◁

# Salt in food – what do you need to know?

The chemical name for salt is **sodium chloride** (NaCl). Both sodium and chloride are needed to keep the concentration of body fluids constant, for a variety of chemical reactions, and chloride is needed for the production of hydrochloric acid in the stomach.

People tend to like the flavour of salt, and consequently the average person in Britain eats **20 times** as much as he or she needs. Too much sodium can lead to high blood pressure in some people, which is one of the factors leading to heart attacks and strokes. It also puts a strain on the kidneys which have the job of maintaining fluid levels in the body. Many processed foods have salt added, and some, such as potato snacks, roasted peanuts, and meat products, are very salty.

There is a need to reduce the amount of salt in the diet, but because our taste buds are accustomed to a salty flavour, it may take several weeks to 'wean' us on to a lower salt intake.

## > Things to do

**1** Use a variety of alternative flavours to salt (e.g. herbs, spices like cumin and coriander, or tomato puree, garlic puree, red pepper and celery) to flavour a basic savoury minced beef recipe.
Set up a tasting panel, and ask 10 people to try a spoonful of mixture from each pan, taking a sip of water in between each. Ask them to give each a score for flavour out of 5 (5 = liked most). Add up the scores at the end (maximum 50 for each mixture), and comment on the results. Which was the most liked? Could you use any other flavours?

**2** Water softening equipment is used in many houses, where the area has hard water. In the process of softening, a salt is used at relatively high concentrations. Why must this water **not** be used to make up bottles of powdered milk to feed a baby?
Why is cows' milk specially modified when it is prepared for sale as human baby powdered milk? Why are parents warned **not** to add more powdered milk to a bottle than stated on the packet?

**3** Study the labels of some low sodium alternatives to ordinary salt. Chemically, how are they different from sodium chloride?

**4** Sodium is found in other chemicals and additives used in foods. Find out which additives it is found in, and compile a list of foods that contain them.

**5** If you were told to reduce your sodium (salt) intake, why would you need to reduce the amount of baked goods where baking powder has been used as a raising agent? ◁

# Fibre in food – what do you need to know?

If you have no difficulty in getting rid of solid waste products (faeces) from your body, you are eating enough fibre. The consequences of not eating enough fibre have been well publicized – problems of constipation and piles (haemhorroids) are common, but are not subjects that people like to discuss with their friends very much!

## What is fibre?

Study the photographs below. They show cross-sections of plant foods that have been magnified. Each photograph shows that the plants are composed of individual **cells**, which vary in shape and size according to their position in the plant, and the type of plant.

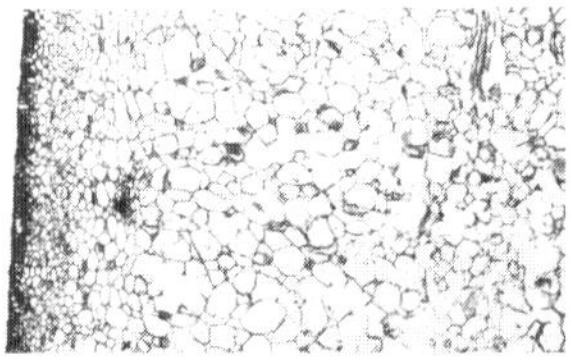
Nectarine (×14)

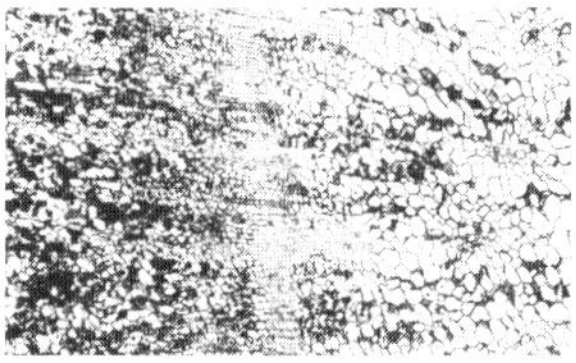
Carrot (×14)

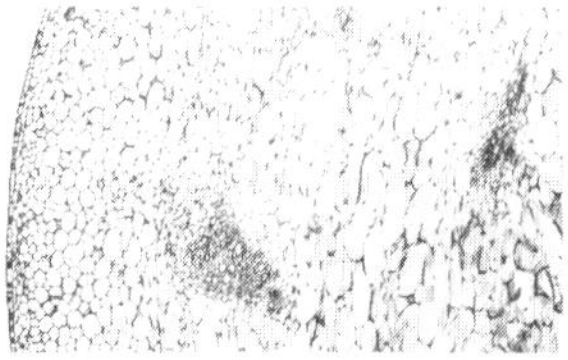
Cucumber (×14)

All the cells have the same basic structure, as shown in the diagram opposite. The **cell walls** are made of a variety of substances, including **cellulose**, **pectin**, **lignin**, and **gums**. All these are given the general name **dietary fibre** (fibre for short). During digestion, we cannot break down the fibre, so it travels through our intestines unchanged. This makes the faeces **bulky**. The **water** in the cells helps to make the faeces **soft**.

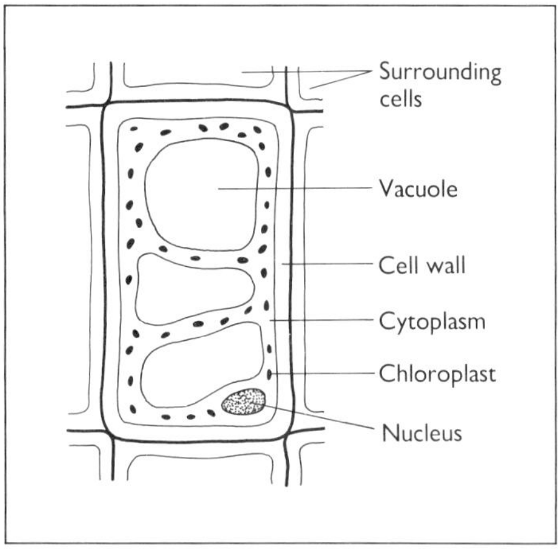


## Which foods will provide fibre?

As all plant foods are composed of cells before they are processed, they are sources of fibre. Some will have more fibre than others, depending on the type of plant, and how much processing they undergo.

**Fruit and vegetables** (especially fresh ones) are of great value because they contain good supplies of fibre in their cell walls and lots of water in the many cells they contain.

**Cereals** (wheat, rice, oats, etc.) are of great value, especially if they are whole grain (unrefined). This is because the outer layers of cereal grains contain thick-walled cells with lots of cellulose in them. There is also cellulose in the cell walls of other cells inside the grain. Cereals, however, contain less water than fruits and vegetables.

## ▷ Things to do

**1** Make a survey of foods that contain fibre (either naturally or added during processing), e.g. baked goods, breakfast cereals, fibre capsules, fruits and vegetables. Work out how much the fibre in the food costs in each case, in the following way. (Check the fibre contents per 100 g, either from the nutritional label or from food tables.)

Fresh apple
Amount of fibre = 2 g for 100 g of apple
Cost of apple = 12p for 150 g of apple

$$\therefore \quad 2\text{ g fibre costs } 12\text{p} \times \frac{100}{150} = 8\text{p}$$

$$\therefore \quad 2\text{ g fibre costs } 8\text{p}$$

Compare the costs of fibre from a variety of of sources in this way. Dietary guidelines suggest that adults should eat 30 g of fibre per day in order to prevent intestinal problems. From your price survey, suggest some interesting and economical ways that people could achieve that goal.

Why do you think that some fibre rich foods, such as wholemeal bread, cost more to buy than similar foods, e.g. white bread?

**2** Using a microscope and glass slides, examine thin cross-sections of a variety of plant foods. Compare the thicknesses of the cell walls in fruits, vegetables and cereals, and from different parts of a plant (e.g. compare the skin with the flesh of a fruit). What did you find?

What implications does this have on the way fruits and vegetables should be prepared?

**3** Investigate a variety of processed foods that emphasize the fibre content of the product. Do they also meet other dietary goal recommendations? Comment on this. How many of them use bran as the extra fibre content?

**4** Whole grain cereals are used by many people to increase their fibre intake. Answer the following questions about this group of foods.

**a** Phytic acid is found in cereal foods. Why might this cause concern if a person's diet was largely composed of whole grain cereals?

**b** Why are whole grain cereal products such as flour more likely to go 'off' quite quickly? ◁

# Dental health

## The structure of a tooth

The photograph below shows a greatly magnified section of the surface of a tooth.

The surface is composed of millions of tiny mineral crystals. The main mineral in them is **calcium**. The minerals in the crystals are constantly dissolved from the tooth and replaced again, because the tooth is a living part of the body.

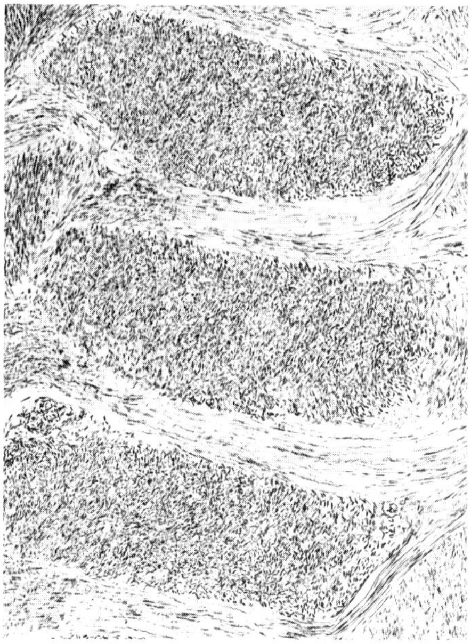

The saliva in the mouth is rich in minerals, including calcium. Saliva is normally **neutral** and constantly washes the teeth. By doing so, it maintains the continual removal and replacement of minerals from the surface of the teeth.

## How is the structure of the tooth weakened?

The bacteria which live on the surface of the teeth, especially in **plaque** (the film of food and bacterial residues which builds up on the teeth), turn carbohydrate (especially sugar) into acids. Acids make minerals dissolve from the teeth more quickly than they can be replaced. The acids **demineralize** the teeth. This causes parts of the tooth surface to become weak. Eventually the weak spots become tiny holes, which enlarge until the whole tooth is weakened by the **cavity** which forms under its surface.

## Can tooth decay be prevented?

Tooth decay and gum disease are extremely common, and the teeth are at their most vulnerable when they are developing in babies and children.

**Fluoride** is a mineral found naturally in some water supplies and in some foods (e.g. fish, green vegetables). It is also added to many different brands of toothpaste. Porous weak spots on the surface of teeth are able to absorb and concentrate fluoride. Research has shown that this helps the tooth to **remineralize**, and helps to prevent further decay.

Prevention of tooth decay is achieved by regular and thorough cleaning and by the consumption of foods rich in mineral elements. A limited intake of sweet foods also helps. It has been shown that the saliva becomes acidic for up to an hour after sweet foods are eaten. During this time, decay will take place.

## Things to do

1 Study the graph below, which shows the acid level in the mouth after eating a food containing sugar.

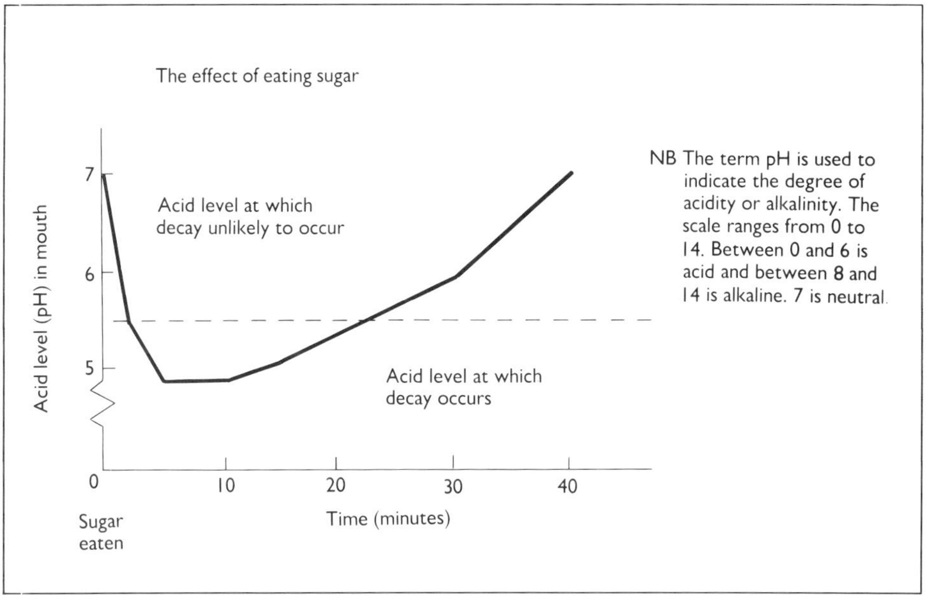


Answer the following questions:

**a** How long after sugar is eaten does the pH level in the mouth return to neutral?

**b** How long does it take after sugar is eaten for the acid level in the mouth to reach its highest point?

**c** why is it advisable to limit the number of **times** in a day when sweet foods are eaten?

**d** Why are boiled sweets and sweets which you chew for a long time particularly bad for teeth?

2 Prepare an informative poster that gives advice to parents about giving their children sweets. Remember to include safety aspects as well as dental health advice

3 Several studies have shown that children who live in areas where the water supply has a natural fluoride content have fewer decayed teeth than those who live in areas with a little or no fluoride in the water.

Find out about fluoridation of water supplies, and the arguments for and against this form of preventative health care.

# *Food for today's consumer*

At all stages of life, people have different requirements (needs) which they aim to satisfy, e.g. requirements associated with the home, clothing, feeding, and leisure. In the case of food, many of us have the following requirements:

- We want quick, easy-to-prepare food.
- We want food that is well presented so that it is appetizing.
- We want satisfying food with a predictable appearance, flavour and texture.
- We want healthy and hygienic food.

## Designing food

**Design** is a means of solving a problem, where there is an identifiable requirement (need). In the case of food, an example of this was the need to produce a cheaper and suitable alternative to butter. This eventually led to the production of margarine.

Food manufacturers use a **design process** to help them develop and produce new food products. Today, there is a vast range of food products available to suit our many different requirements. Social factors and our style of living have changed in recent years, and these have influenced the design of new foods.

### How have we changed?

- We spend less time preparing food.
- We do less manual work and have more machines to work for us.
- We have more leisure time.
- We eat more meals out of the home.
- We know more about food and health.

Food manufacturers conduct **market research** when they are developing a new product. This involves interviewing people to find out about their requirements and opinions, and asking them to complete questionnaires which provide the manufacturer with more detailed information. Once a product has been developed, **tasting panels** are organized, and people are asked to sample the food and **evaluate** it for factors such as flavour, colour, and texture. The results of the evaluation are then used to further develop the product if necessary. The manufacturer may then conduct a **trial run**, by selling the product in a limited number of shops in one or two areas of the country. **Advertising** the product will encourage people to try it, and this will be aimed at a particular group of people. If the product sells well, then the manufacturer will **distribute** it to other areas, using a **promotion campaign** to encourage sales. The whole process may take several months.

## Solving a problem

Set out below is a problem (sometimes called a **brief**) that could be given to a food technologist to solve:

| |
|---|
| Design an alternative cream cake, that will satisfy the requirements of and be attractive to someone on a slimming diet. |

Here is an example of one way of approaching the problem:

**1** List the requirements that a slimmer would have.

- **a** appetizing food to satisfy the desire for a cake when on a slimming diet
- **b** low fat and carbohydrate (especially sugar) content in food
- **c** food with a low energy value (low calorie, see page 23)

**2** What do cream cakes usually consist of?

sugar – in the sponge mixture and in jam or chocolate used for filling and decoration

fat – in the sponge mixture and in cream used for filling and decoration, and in nuts and chocolate

flour and eggs – in the sponge mixture

**3** What suitable alternative products are available with lower energy values?

low sugar jams, canned fruits without added sugar

low fat spreads (margarine and butter substitutes – but some cannot be used in baked foods)

reduced fat creams

4 Some suggestions for solving the problem are given below (they may involve some practical work and tasting panels):

| Suggestion | Evaluation |
|---|---|
| Use less fat in the sponge mixture | May affect the texture of the cake. |
| Use a whisked sponge mixture instead of a creamed one | Reduces fat content considerably, but sponge texture may be dry. |
| Use only egg whites (not yolks) | Should set the mixture, but give a paler coloured sponge. |
| Reduce the sugar content of sponge mixture | May affect how much air is trapped, but some reduction should be possible. |
| Use low fat cream | May not whip up enough for piped decoration, but could be used for filling. |
| Use more fruit for the filling and decoration to add bulk to the cake | Would enhance the appearance of the cake but too much may make it too moist. |

5 Calculate the energy value of the chosen alternative cake, using food tables. Compare it with the usual cake recipe.
Use this information to help promote the product.

6 Produce the final product, and test its suitability by conducting trial sales in a number of food shops.
Advertise the product intensively to encourage people to try it.

7 Evaluate the success of the product, and adapt it if necessary. Obviously, the method of solving a problem varies, according to what the problem is. However, the principle is the same – approaching the problem logically, and developing, testing and reassessing your solutions all the way along. On the opposite page are some problems for you to tackle. Try to apply your knowledge about food to any that you answer.

## ▷ Things to do

1 Study the photographs of different packaging methods used for a variety of foods.

Ring-pull can

Squeezy sauce bottle

Carton

In each case, answer the questions below:

- **a** What do you think was the original design problem identified by food technologists that led them to the production of each item? (e.g. What were the disadvantages of being unable to open a can of drink without a can opener?)
- **b** Which group of people do you think each product might have been aimed at in particular ?
- **c** List some food products that use each method of packaging.

2 What requirements might the following groups of people have, that should be considered by a food manufacturer who is developing a product for them?

- **a** babies being weaned on to solid foods (and their parents who will prepare the food and give it to them)
- **b** people (of all ages) who are trying to follow dietary guidelines and want a range of healthy but interesting meals
- **c** children who would like to have snack foods included in their packed school lunches

3 What are the main forms of advertising used for food products? As a consumer, what information would you like a food advertisement to give you, and which types of advertisement do you disagree with (give examples and reasons in your answer)?

4 **Practical problem to solve.**
You have been asked to prepare a two course lunch for two senior citizens. The gentleman has heart disease,and so has to limit his intake of saturated fat and salt. The lady is lacto-vegetarian. You are limited by time to one hour, and have access to only a hob and grill to cook on. Design a meal to solve this practical problem. Show how you have thought the process through, and why you discarded some solutions that you arrived at on the way.

This type of problem confronts many people who have the job of preparing food for others. Why is good organization important in solving such problems? ◁

# Fast food

## What does 'fast food' mean?

Fast food comes in many forms, from mushy peas to take-away curry. Fast food restaurants and shops are a feature of modern living, where people can:

- buy a meal or snack from a limited range offered by the restaurant, shop or stall
- eat it easily and quickly either inside or outside
- and dispose of the packaging it was served in afterwards.

Many fast food restaurants are modelled on those found in the USA, and have the following features:

- They sell a limited, but popular, range of foods using standardized recipes, with predictable flavours and appearances.
- The food is usually prepared in a factory, then distributed to several outlets.
- Staff need minimum training.
- They are often open late at night and on Sundays.
- They use disposable cutlery, plates, etc., and have easy-to-maintain interior decorations and furnishings.
- They are often used as social meeting places.
- They cater for families and often offer party facilities.

Fast food restaurants therefore offer a variety of facilities that are popular with many people. However, their effect on the local environment can give rise to concern.

## Things to do

1 List the design features and properties of the materials used for packaging take-away foods.
Can you suggest any improvements that could be made to the packaging (e.g. could less be used, could the shapes of the packaging be improved)?

2 Using food tables for reference, comment on the suggestion that fast foods are 'junk' foods.

3 Find out what Chinese Restaurant Syndrome is (clue – it is an illness which affects some people who often eat Chinese food).

4 Why are microwave cookers such a useful piece of equipment for take-away restaurants? How do they help in the prevention of food poisoning?

5 How do you think fast food take-away restaurants could help in a campaign to stop people dropping litter in the streets?

6 What features and facilities do some fast food restaurants have to make them attractive to families with young children?

7 Using the telephone directory to help you, list the types of fast food restaurant that are open in your home area. Comment on whether you think they are an important or necessary facility in your area.

# Preparing and cooking food

For the preparation and cooking of food to be an enjoyable and satisfying activity, it is useful to have an understanding of the changes that take place in foods. Such knowledge is useful for several reasons:

- You can avoid future mistakes.
- You can produce good results with minimum effort and maximum efficiency.

- You can usually provide an explanation if something does fail.
- You can adapt recipes to suit your own requirements.

- You avoid the need to constantly refer to recipe books for guidance.

- You can spend money wisely on food, e.g. by understanding how best to cook less expensive meat cuts.
- You can make full use of kitchen technology to save time and energy on a variety of processes.

On the following pages, you will find some charts listing the main changes that take place in foods during preparation and cooking. The charts describe individual changes that occur, but in practice, a food may undergo several changes at the same time, e.g. during baking, a cake will rise, develop a crust, and change in texture from being moist and soft to becoming relatively dry and spongy.

# Changes in foods during preparation

| What happens | Reasons | Find out |
|---|---|---|
| Food changes colour, e.g. | | |
| • red meat turns brown when stored | **Oxymyoglobin** in meat makes it red. It changes to **metmyoglobin** if stored in a place with little oxygen available. | **1** Why you should remove cling film from fresh meat before storing it in the refrigerator. |
| • some cut fruits – apples, bananas etc. – go brown | **Enzymes** in the fruit react with oxygen in the air, and the surface goes brown. The process is called **oxidation**. | **2** Why the addition of lemon juice to cut fruit prevents the change in colour. |
| Food loses some of its nutritional value, e.g. | | |
| • vitamin C (ascorbic acid) | Vitamin C is **oxidized** by exposure to air. This changes its chemical structure so that it cannot be used by the body. It is also dissolved by water. | **3** Why it is bad practice to cut up vegetables or fruit a long time before they are eaten. |
| • vitamin A (retinol) | Vitamin A is destroyed by exposure to light. | **4** Why cartons of long life milk are lined with metal foil. |
| • vitamin $B_2$ (riboflavin) | Vitamin $B_2$ is destroyed by exposure to light. | **5** Why it is good practice to bring milk in from outside soon after it is delivered. |
| Food is partially tenderized, e.g. meat, by | | |
| • pounding and scoring | Pounding and scoring reduces the length of the muscle fibres. | **6** Which cuts of meat can be treated in these ways before cooking. |
| • using meat tenderizer powder | Tenderizing powder contains **enzymes** which partially digest the meat protein. | |
| • marinading in vinegar or alcohol | Marinading in acid or alcohol partially coagulates the meat proteins. | |

## Changes in food during preparation (contd.)

| What happens | Reasons |
|---|---|
| Food increases in size, e.g. | |
| • dried fruit or pulses soaked in water | Water passes into the fruit or pulse as a result of **osmosis**. The water causes the cells inside to swell, thus making the fruit or pulse larger. |
| • bread dough | Yeast in the dough produces carbon dioxide ($CO_2$) gas, which makes the dough rise. |
| • whipped egg white | The protein **albumin** can stretch and hold up to 7 times its own volume of air. |
| Food becomes thicker, e.g. | |
| • mayonnaise | Egg yolk contains **lecithin** which emulsifies the oil and vinegar and prevents them from separating out. The mixture becomes thickened as the lecithin starts to work. |
| • whipped cream | As cream is whipped, the fat globules it contains start to **coalesce** (stick together), until the cream becomes thick. |
| Food curdles, e.g. | |
| • cake mixture | If egg is added too quickly, the lecithin in the yolk does not have time to stabilize the fat and sugar, so the fat curdles (separates). |
| • milk | The protein **caseinogen** will coagulate and curdle if acid is added. |
| Food absorbs other substances, e.g. | |
| • odours | Odours are absorbed by eggs through their porous shells and by fat-containing foods, e.g. butter. |
| • water | Water is absorbed by some dried foods, e.g. coffee, because they are **hygroscopic** (attract water from the atmosphere). |

**Find out**

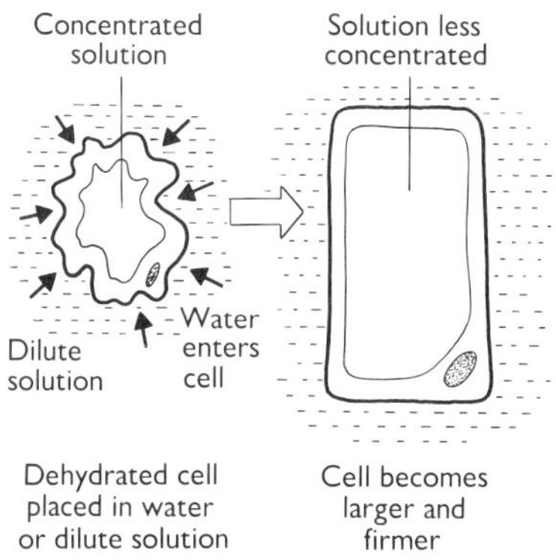


7 Why many pulses must be boiled after soaking.

8 How osmosis destroys harmful organisms in foods which are dehydrated.

9 The conditions yeast requires to produce $CO_2$ gas.

10 Why bread dough must be stretchy.

11 Why overwhipped egg white becomes flat and runny.

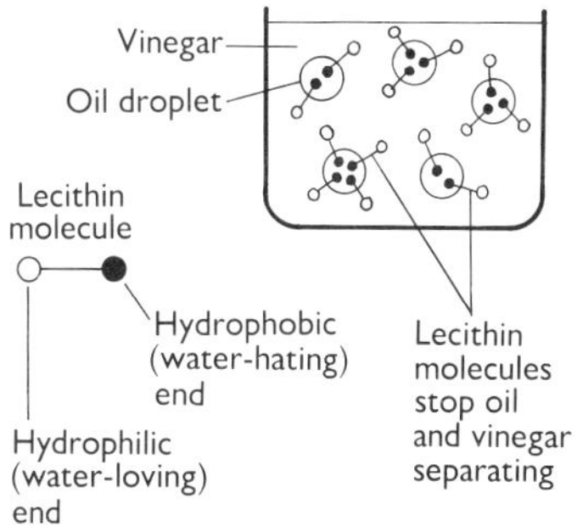


12 Why the oil must not be added too quickly when making mayonnaise.

13 Why single cream will not thicken when whipped.

14 Why a curdled cake mixture may not rise very well during cooking.

15 Why sour milk will curdle when heated.

16 The best ways to store foods in the refrigerator or deep freeze to prevent transfer of odours.

17 The best way to store dried foods.

# Changes in foods during cooking

| What happens | Reasons |
|---|---|
| Mixture enlarges (rises), e.g. bread, cakes, scones | Air is trapped during mixing, or gas is produced by chemical raising agents, or steam is produced from water in the mixture.<br>Air, gas, and steam all expand with heat and push up the mixture during cooking. |
| Food shrinks or loses bulk, e.g. | |
| • meat | Heat makes the protein molecules in meat alter their structure so that they become shorter. The connective tissue becomes shorter and thicker so that the meat shrinks. |
| • leafy vegetables | Boiling breaks down the cell structure in the leaves, so that they become less bulky. |
| Food increases in size, e.g. pasta, rice | These foods contain **starch**, which is located in tiny granules. As they are heated in water, the granules absorb water and swell. Some of them release their starch as heating increases. |
| Food becomes firmer (sets), e.g. | |
| • egg protein | Protein molecules in the white and yolk start to coagulate (become firmer) at about 60 °C and 70 °C respectively. As cooking continues, the whole egg sets. |
| • gelatine | Gelatine absorbs water and swells. When heated, the gelatine dissolves to form a clear liquid which sets when cooled. |

**Find out**

1 What is the importance of **gluten** in these mixtures.

2 Why is it important to have the oven temperature correct.

3 Why joints of meat from the neck and shin parts of animals need long, moist cooking.

4 Why leafy vegetables should be cooked for the minimum time.

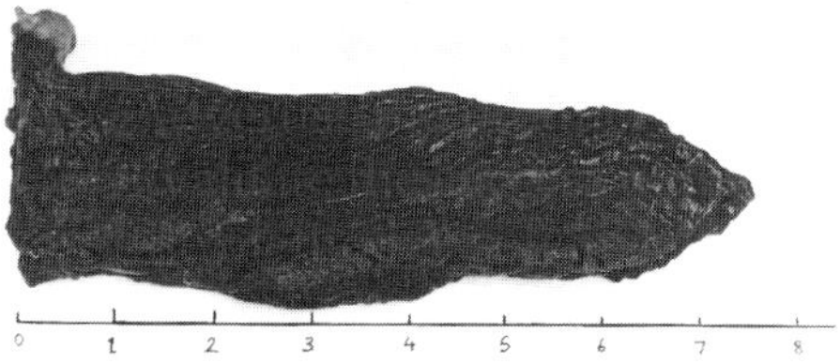


5 Why overcooked rice is sticky.

6 Why whole grain rice takes longer to cook than polished rice.

7 Why overcooked egg protein is tough and indigestible.

8 Why you should not boil gelatine when dissolving the crystals.

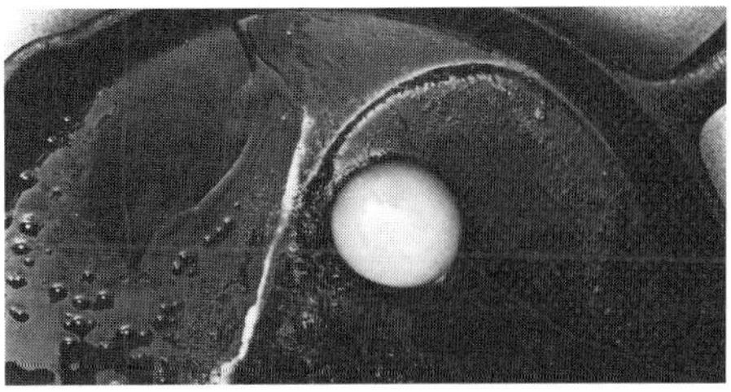

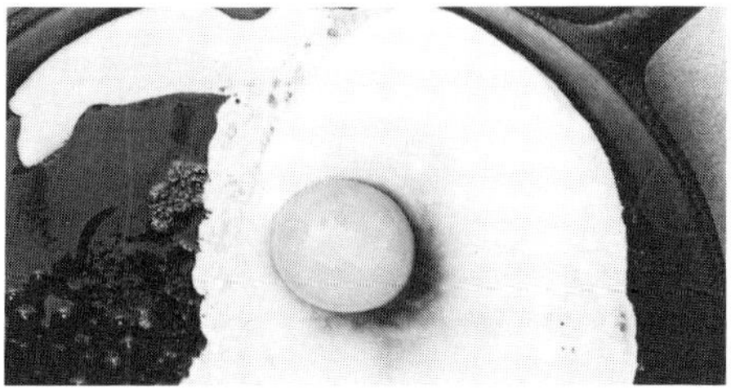

## Changes in foods during cooking (contd.)

| What happens | Reasons | Find out |
| --- | --- | --- |
| Food changes colour, e.g. | | |
| • meat goes brown | **Oxymyoglobin** in uncooked meat makes it red. During cooking it changes to **haemochrome** which is brown. | **9** What makes ham pink. |
| • green vegetables | **Chlorophyll** in green vegetables becomes bright green when the vegetable is first cooked. If overcooked, it changes to olive green/ brown. | **10** Why it is inadvisable to add bicarbonate of soda to green vegetables to make them stay bright green. |
| • sugar | Sugar crystals are white, but on exposure to heat, they gradually become golden brown due to a change in the sugar molecules. This is called **caramelization**. | **11** Why the crusts of bread, cakes, etc. are brown.<br>**12** Why demerara and similar sugars are brown. |
| Food loses some of its nutritional value, e.g. | | |
| • vitamin C (ascorbic acid) | Vitamin C is destroyed by heat. The longer the exposure to heat, the greater the destruction. | **13** Why pressure cooking, microwave cooking and steaming are all good methods of cooking vegetables and fruit. |
| • vitamin $B_1$ (thiamin)<br>• vitamin $B_2$ (riboflavin) | These are both destroyed by exposure to heat. | |
| Food becomes tender when cooked, e.g. | | |
| • meat | Connective tissue becomes shorter and thicker. **Collagen** is converted to gelatine in the presence of moisture. | **14** Why fish is more tender than meat. |
| • rice, pulses, pasta, vegetables and fruit | Water is absorbed into the starch granules, which soften and swell. Some starch escapes from ruptured granules and dissolves. | |
| Food becomes thicker, e.g. cornflour and roux sauces | Both contain starch, located in granules. These soften and swell as they absorb water. Some starch escapes from ruptured granules and dissolves. | **15** Why sauces must be stirred when cooking. |

## ▷ Things to do

Listed below are a variety of practical assignments based on changes that occur in foods during preparation and processing. Use them to prepare illustrated topic work on this aspect of food, and at each stage, note the changes you observe in the individual foods and mixtures that you prepare.

**1** Plan a two-course meal which illustrates the following changes that occur in protein:
- **a** it becomes solid when heated
- **b** it is denatured when exposed to acid
- **c** it is sometimes denatured by mechanical actions such as whisking.

**2** Prepare a two-course meal which illustrates the steps you can take to avoid three of the following:
- **a** browning of cut fruit
- **b** loss of bright green colour of leafy vegetables when cooked
- **c** poor rising of a whisked sponge cake
- **d** poor rising of bread dough
- **e** shrinking of pastry in a savoury flan.

**3** Prepare a light lunch to illustrate how, by careful preparation and cooking, you can provide a nutritionally sound meal for someone recovering from an operation on his or her digestive system.

**4** Prepare a variety of dishes to illustrate the following properties of fats and oils:
- **a** Fats and oils have different smoke points, therefore not all of them can be used for frying.
- **b** Fats are 'plastic' which means that they can be spread easily at a certain temperature.
- **c** Oils do not readily mix with water.
- **d** Some fats have a shortening effect on gluten in flour.

**5** Prepare a variety of dishes to illustrate the following properties of carbohydrate:
- **a** Sugars caramelize when heated to a certain temperature.
- **b** Starch granules swell when heated in water.
- **c** As heating continues, some starch granules rupture, releasing starch. This forms a gel with water, which sets on cooling. ◁

# Efficiency in the kitchen

The design of modern kitchens and much of the equipment in them is geared to saving time and being efficient (carrying out a task with minimum effort and maximum effect).

- Meal preparation no longer requires hours of 'slaving over a hot stove'.
- There are gadgets and machines for all the main processes and jobs in the kitchen.
- Even washing up afterwards can be virtually effortless . . .
  . . . providing you understand how to use the technology.

Efficiency is not just a matter of machines and gadgets. Thoughtful, tidy, and reasonably fast practical work, by the people preparing the food, means that they have more time to enjoy the food they have produced. As there are so many items available for use in the kitchen, it is a good exercise to do a little consumer research before you buy a particular piece of equipment designed to save you time. Listed below are some examples of questions you might find it useful to have the answers to, when choosing a piece of kitchen equipment:

1. Does the machine/gadget do exactly what you want it to?
2. Will it do other jobs as well?
3. Is it easy to operate?
4. Will it take up a lot of space?
5. Is it easy to clean and maintain?
6. Will you use it enough to justify spending the money on it?
7. Does it have good safety features?

## ▷ Things to do

**1** Many items of equipment are tested and compared with similar models for their efficiency, safety, cost, special features, etc., and the results are published in consumer magazines and journals. It is useful to study these results if you are choosing an item of equipment. Below is part of a chart showing the results of some tests on food processors. Answer the questions that follow it:

| Model | Guarantee period | Weight | Features | Controls | Blending celery soup (*smoothness score 1-5*) | Wastage loss % | | | |
|---|---|---|---|---|---|---|---|---|---|
| | | | | | | Grating cheese | Slicing pepper | Slicing cucumber fine | Slicing cucumber thick |
| Braun Multipractic MC1V | 1 year | 2.22 kg | Nonslip feet, cable storage, handle on bowl | 3 settings – switch off pulsator continuous action | 2 | 3% | 82% | 91% | 98% |
| Krups Rotary 500 | 1 year | 3.85 kg | Non-slip feet, cable storage, tinted bowl, plunger graduated for measuring, handle on bowl | 4 settings – off, pulsator, low and high speed | 3 | 13% | 24% | 1% | 60% |

**a** Which food processor was
 **i** most efficient at slicing a cucumber thinly
 **ii** least efficient at slicing green pepper
 **iii** least efficient at producing a smooth textured soup
 **iv** most efficient at grating cheese?

**b** List the safety features of each food processor.

**c** Why might the weight of each food processor be an important feature?

**d** What do guarantees usually protect the consumer against?

**2** Microwave cookers are a common feature of modern kitchens. As a group, conduct a survey among people who own a microwave cooker, and find out why they bought a microwave, what they use it for mainly, what features they like about it, how much time it saves them, etc. Prepare a report based on your results, and display your findings. In your conclusion, comment on how useful you might find a microwave cooker if you were running your own home.

**3** What types of convenience foods (give examples) might you buy if you were in each of the following situations:

**a** a working parent with two school age children

**b** a single person with a job that entails some shift work

**c** a widowed pensioner with an active social and hobbies life?

**4** Make a survey of a variety of small kitchen gadgets (e.g. orange peeler, bean slicer, salad spinner, garlic crusher). If possible, use some of these for the job they were intended for, and compare them for time, ease of use, clearing up, etc. with doing the same job by hand using just a knife or colander, etc.
What are your general conclusions about kitchen gadgets?

**5** If you were in a position to buy a large item of time and labour saving equipment, give details of what you would buy, and justify why it would be valuable to you. ◁

# The end of the food chain

Look back to the information about the food chain on page 10. The last part of the food chain involves the disposal of waste products, and the decay of dead animals and plants. As these are broken down during the decay process, the nutrients they contain are released into the soil and water, ready to be used for the growth of more plants.

Domestic waste (mostly food and packaging waste) is only one of several groups of waste products that have to be disposed of. Other groups of rubbish include:

sewage
industrial waste (chemicals, packaging, spent fuel etc.)
food manufacturing waste
over-produced crops of vegetables and fruits

Disposing of the vast quantities of waste products that people produce is expensive, sometimes dangerous, time consuming, and often causes disagreement between industry and environmentalists about the best method of disposal.

## Packaging

Most foods (like many other products) are packaged before being sold. Packaging serves several purposes:

- It protects the food from physical damage, contamination by micro-organisms, pollution, and atmospheric conditions such as damp.
- It enables food to be easily displayed in a shop.
- It gives consumers information about the food inside.

Food packaging is a large part of the food industry (see page 45). For example, more than 6000 million canned foods are sold in the UK every year. Each of those cans has to be manufactured, labelled and packed into boxes or polythene wrap for distribution to food shops. The main groups of materials used to package food are **plastics**, **glass**, **metal**, **paper** and **cardboard**. These materials account for 40–45 per cent of the total weight of domestic waste in the UK.

There are two groups of people in the packaging industry who control the supply information to the government and public about food packaging. They are the Industry Committee for Packaging and the Environment (INCPEN) and the Packaging Council. They have a code of practice which manufacturers of packaging are encouraged to follow.

The code has several clauses including:

The packaging must not mislead the public about the quantity, size or type of contents.

The packaging must be convenient to handle and use.

The packaging must clearly show relevant information about the product.

The packaging must not adversely affect the contents inside.

The packaging must be produced with due consideration to the environment.

## ▷ Things to do

**1** Study the photographs of different types of packaging below. Comment on how each has benefited the consumer:

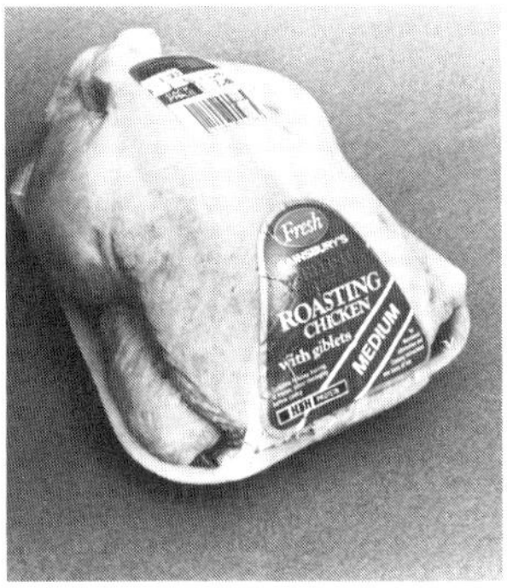

**2** With safety, convenience and ease of use in mind, list the design requirements for the packaging of foods and household chemicals for these groups of people:
**a** elderly people
**b** children and babies
**c** disabled people (blind, arthritic, wheelchair bound)
Give examples which you have seen yourself in your answer.

**3** Why was there concern recently about the use of cling film to wrap foods?

**4** Study a variety of labels on foods with different types of packaging. Which ones attracted you most? Can you say why this was? Would you prefer to see plain and simple labels on foods?

**5** Which types of packaging do you find the most frustrating to open and dispose of? Can you suggest any improvements you would like to see, to make them easier to use?

**6** Over the course of a week, note down the number and types of packaging items you and your family dispose of. At the end of the week, add up the total, and the total for each type of packaging (glass, plastic, metal, paper/cardboard). Comment on your results. Compare your results with other people's in your class, and present your class findings as part of a display on packaging and waste.

**7** What are the reasons for the following advice?
**a** Unwrap fresh meat from its plastic covering and place in a covered glass dish in a cool place.
**b** 'Once opened, place these biscuits in an airtight container.'
**c** 'Once opened, store any leftovers from this can of fruit in a glass or plastic container.'
**d** Do not buy badly dented or rusted cans of food.
**e** 'Once opened, store this jar of fish or meat paste in a cool place and use within three days.'
**f** 'Once opened, treat this carton of UHT milk as fresh milk.' ◁

# Wasting food

Food is wasted by people in several ways, e.g.

peeling vegetables and fruits too thickly
failing to consume a perishable product before it starts to decay
poor storage of food, so that it becomes mouldy or attacked by pests
over catering for a particular number of people
buying more food than can be eaten at one time
over-producing certain crops

Food wastage raises many moral questions, because there are so many people in the world who are starving, yet food wastage is high in countries where there is plenty. It is an issue to which there is no simple answer, but one which should not be pushed out of the way.

## Things to do

1 Over a period of a week, write down on a chart every time you throw away an item of food. Indicate whether it was inedible waste (e.g. peelings, bones, etc.) or not.
At the end of the week, study your chart and suggest ways in which you could have cut down on the waste, e.g. did you really need to peel every fruit or vegetable?

2 Find out where the leftover food from the school canteen is sent. Are there any rules about its disposal?

3 How can food waste be used in the garden? What products can you buy to help speed up the process of rotting down food waste?

4 'Waste not, want not' is a saying you may have heard before. It was often displayed on a poster in large Victorian kitchens for all the kitchen maids to see. Write an essay about how you can make use of leftover foods, and the possible dangers this may involve. How has modern technology benefited people in preparing meals using leftovers?

# Quiz – How do you rate as a food consumer?

Read the questions below, and choose one of the answers in each case. Think about them before you answer, and be as honest as possible. At the end, add up your score from the chart on page 2 to see how you rate.

**1** Do you wash vegetables and fruits before you prepare and eat them?
A never
B sometimes
C always

**2** Do you ever go shopping for food either on your own or to help someone else out?
A often
B seldom
C never

**3** Are you aware of the current prices of the following basic foods: bread, milk, cheddar cheese, eggs, and potatoes?
A do not know any
B know only 1 or 2
C know almost all or all

**4** How often do you read the information supplied on a food label?
A never
B seldom
C often

**5** Do you try new food products and compare them with other foods, when you can?
A never
B seldom
C often

**6** Do you plan, prepare and cook the meals in your home?
A never
B seldom
C often

# Word search

Listed below are the clues to help you solve the word search on this page. Turn to page 2 for the answers. All the words appear somewhere in the book.

1. These feed the soil.
2. These eat plants and animals.
3. Milk sold in silver topped bottles is processed in this way.
4. The process by which solid fat is made from liquid oil.
5. If you want to find out what is in the food you have bought, read this.
6. The process of adding nutrients to a food that are not naturally present in it.
7. Another name for glucose.
8. Food that is easily and quickly bought and eaten.
9. This protects food from damage and contamination.
10. A company that makes food products.
11. This is denatured by heat, acids, and mechanical methods.
12. An additive used to stop oils from separating out of food.
13. This might raise your blood pressure.
14. All food starts with this – without it, there would be no life.
15. This word means that a substance contains carbon.

NB The words may be found horizontally, vertically, or diagonally.

| | | | | | | | | | | | | | | | | | | | | | |
|---|---|---|---|---|---|---|---|---|---|---|---|---|---|---|---|---|---|---|---|---|---|
| M | A | N | U | F | A | C | T | U | R | E | R | F | E | D | G | H | N | L | N | P | W |
| P | F | R | Q | O | M | E | N | O | T | I | B | G | L | N | E | I | J | K | X | O | N |
| Z | O | A | E | M | L | K | A | F | Z | X | R | S | F | E | F | X | T | P | T | S | W |
| V | S | T | L | N | G | L | D | L | W | P | O | U | G | T | M | F | T | F | Q | X | V |
| F | E | R | T | I | L | I | Z | E | R | S | I | N | C | M | A | A | M | R | S | N | T |
| O | S | W | L | V | F | Q | N | R | S | T | U | H | M | T | P | S | D | M | O | C | S |
| R | B | Y | C | O | G | P | M | F | A | S | T | F | O | O | D | S | S | I | V | S | R |
| T | D | A | D | R | H | O | L | V | W | X | T | L | S | T | S | J | T | P | N | E | E |
| I | F | C | L | E | I | J | K | Y | Z | N | O | T | H | O | T | A | Z | T | D | H | M |
| F | H | P | A | S | T | E | U | R | I | Z | A | T | I | O | N | G | H | O | T | B | U |
| I | J | E | B | C | O | N | Z | H | J | L | A | I | O | E | O | N | F | R | W | T | L |
| C | L | G | E | E | E | C | T | N | E | C | F | R | G | A | I | R | E | G | L | V | S |
| A | N | I | L | N | A | L | T | P | N | P | R | O | T | E | I | N | L | A | T | R | I |
| T | P | K | R | D | A | A | I | A | N | T | R | E | I | T | E | Y | C | N | T | H | F |
| I | R | M | N | S | S | Q | Z | F | R | D | L | U | S | E | O | I | V | I | U | N | I |
| O | T | O | A | O | A | P | T | N | Y | O | E | J | G | H | P | T | S | C | V | O | E |
| N | V | P | D | N | A | R | N | H | M | Z | R | P | A | C | K | A | G | I | N | G | R |

# Index


acid, in mouth 41
additives 24–5

carnivores 10
changes in foods 49–54
Common Agricultural Policy 15

designing food 42–3

E numbers 24
efficiency 56–7
energy 31, 33
enriching food 23

fast food 46–7
fat 20, 22, 31–3
fatty acids 20, 33
fertilizers 13
fibre 38–9
food
  chain 10–11, 58
  industry 5
  labels 25
  manufacturers 5, 23
  production 12–15
  surpluses 15
fortification 23

herbicides 11
herbivores 10
hydrogenation 33

insecticides 11

kitchens 56

market research 43
minerals (in teeth) 40

nitrate 13
nutrients 30
  effect of processing on 22
nutrition labels 20–21, 23, 34

omnivores 10
organic food 14

packaging 58–60
pesticides 11
photosynthesis 10
preparing food 48–51
processing food 18–19

restoring (nutrient content of food) 23

salt 37
sugar 34–6

teeth 40

vitamins 22, 49, 54

wastage 61
water 28–9